A BEGINNERS' GUIDE TO

2D PUZZLE GAMES WITH UNITY

Create simple 2D puzzle games and learn to code in the process

Patrick Felicia

A BEGINNER'S GUIDE TO

2D PUZZLE GAMES

WITH UNITY

First published: March 2017

Published by Patrick Felicia

CREDITS

Author: Patrick Felicia

ABOUT THE AUTHOR

Patrick Felicia is a <u>lecturer and researcher</u> at Waterford Institute of Technology, where he teaches and supervises undergraduate and postgraduate students. He obtained his MSc in Multimedia Technology in 2003 and PhD in Computer Science in 2009 from University College Cork, Ireland. He has published several books and articles on the use of video games for educational purposes, including the Handbook of Research on Improving Learning and Motivation through Educational Games: Multidisciplinary Approaches (published by IGI), and Digital Games in Schools: a Handbook for Teachers, published by European Schoolnet. Patrick is also the Editor-in-chief of the <u>International Journal of Game-Based Learning (IJGBL),</u> and the Conference Director of the <u>Irish Conference on Game-Based Learning</u>, a popular conference on games and learning organized throughout Ireland.

SUPPORT AND RESOURCES FOR THIS BOOK

To complete the activities presented in this book you need to download the startup pack on the companion website; it consists of free resources that you will need to complete your projects, including bonus material that will help you along the way (e.g., cheat sheets, introductory videos, code samples, and much more).

- Please open the following link: http://learntocreategames.com/books/

- Select the corresponding book.

- On the new page, click on the link labelled "Book Files", or scroll down to the bottom of the page.

- In the section called "**Download your Free Resource Pack**", enter your email address and your first name, and click on the button labeled "**Yes, I want to receive my bonus pack**".

- After a few seconds, you should receive a link to your free start-up pack.

- When you receive the link, you can download all the resources to your computer.

This book is dedicated to Helena

TABLE OF CONTENTS

PREFACE

After teaching Unity for over 5 years, I always thought it could be great to find a book that could get my students started with Unity in a few hours and that showed them how to master the core functionalities offered by this fantastic software.

Many of the books that I found were too short and did not provide enough details on the reasons behind the actions recommended and taken; other books were highly theoretical, and I found that they lacked practicality and that they would not get my students' full attention. In addition, I often found that game development may be preferred by those with a programming background, but that people with an Arts background, even if they wanted to get to know how to create games, often had to face the challenge of learning to code for the first time.

As a result, I started to consider a format that would cover both aspects: be approachable (even to the students with no programming background), keep students highly motivated and involved using an interesting project, cover the core functionalities available in Unity to get started with game programming, provide answers to common questions, and also provide, if need be, a considerable amount of details for some topics.

I then created a book series entitled **Unity From Zero to Proficiency** that did just that. It gave readers the opportunity to discover Unity's core features, especially those that would make it possible to create an interesting 3D game rapidly. After reading this book series, many readers emailed me to let me know how the book series helped them; however, they also mentioned that they wanted to be able to create a simple game from start to finish, publish it and share it with their friends.

This is the reason why I created this new book series entitled "**A Beginner's guide**"; it is for people who already have completed the first four books in the series called **Unity From Zero to Proficiency**, and who would like to focus on a particular aspect of their game development. This being said, this new book series assumes no prior knowledge on the part of the reader, and it will get you started quickly on a particular aspect of Unity.

In this book, focused on 2D puzzle games, you will be completing four 2D puzzle games and also code in C#. By completing each chapter, and by following step-by-step instructions, you will progressively create four complete 2D puzzle games and learn more about C# programming in the process.

You will also create a 2D game that includes many of the common techniques found in puzzle games including: generating random words or cards, making it possible for the player to drag and drop pieces (e.g., cards), playing and recording a sequence of keys pressed by the player, playing sound effects, processing users' choices, or keeping track of the score.

CONTENT COVERED BY THIS BOOK

Chapter 1, Creating a Word Guessing Game, shows you how to create a simple word guessing game where the player has to find the letters that make-up a word chosen at random. You will learn to create a user interface for the game, to read words from a text file, and to pick one word from the file randomly. You will also learn how to process the player's input.

Chapter 2, Creating a Memory Game, shows you how to create a game where the player has to memorize and to play an increasing sequence of colors and sounds, in a similar way as the **Simon** game that was popular in the 80s. You will learn how to create and generate audio within Unity and change the sounds' frequency, to detect when a player has pressed a button, to generate colors at random, and also to record the sequence entered by the player and then compare it to the correct sequence.

Chapter 3, Creating a Card Guessing Game, shows you how to create a card game where the player has to match cards after memorizing their location. You will learn how to change the texture of a sprite at run-time, check when two cards picked by the player are similar, and also how to shuffle cards.

Chapter 4, Creating a Puzzle Game, shows how to create a puzzle game where the player needs to move pieces in the right location to complete a puzzle. Along the way, you will learn how to slice an image into several sprites (i.e., pieces) to create puzzle pieces from an image of your choice, and how to shuffle these puzzle pieces; you will also learn how to make it possible for the player to move (i.e., drag and drop) these pieces, to make these pieces "snap" to a particular location, and to detect when the player has dragged and dropped a piece to the correct location.

Chapter 5 provides answers to Frequently Asked Questions (FAQs) related to the topics covered in this book.

Chapter 6 summarizes the topics covered in this book and provides you with more information on the next steps.

WHAT YOU NEED TO USE THIS BOOK

To complete the project presented in this book, you only need Unity 5.5 (or a more recent version) and to also ensure that your computer and its operating system comply with Unity's requirements. Unity can be downloaded from the official website (http://www.unity3d.com/download), and before downloading it, you can check that your computer is up to scratch on the following page: http://www.unity3d.com/unity/system-requirements. At the time of writing this book, the following operating systems are supported by Unity for development: Windows XP (i.e., SP2+, 7 SP1+), Windows 8, and Mac OS X 10.6+. In terms of graphics card, most cards produced after 2004 should be suitable.

In terms of computer skills, all knowledge introduced in this book will assume no prior programming experience from the reader. So for now, you only need to be able to perform common computer tasks, such as downloading items, opening and saving files, be comfortable with dragging and dropping items and typing, and be relatively comfortable with Unity's interface. This being said, because the focus of this book is on creating 2D puzzle games, and while all steps are explained step-by-step, you may need to be relatively comfortable with Unity's interface, and with coding in C#, as well as creating and transforming objects.

So, if you would prefer to become more comfortable with Unity and C# programming prior to starting this book, you can download the books in the series called Unity 5 From Zero to Proficiency (Foundations, Beginner, or Intermediate, Advanced). These books cover most of the shortcuts and views available in Unity, as well as how to perform common tasks in Unity, such as creating objects, transforming objects, importing assets, using navigation controllers, creating scripts or exporting the game to the web. They also explain how to code your game using both UnityScript of C# along with good coding practices.

WHO THIS BOOK IS FOR

If you can answer **yes** to all these questions, then this book is for you:

1. Would you like to learn how to create 2D puzzle games?

2. Can you already code in C#?

3. Would you like to discover more 2D features in Unity?

4. Although you may have had some prior exposure to Unity and coding, would you like to delve more into 2D puzzle games?

WHO THIS BOOK IS NOT FOR

If you can answer yes to all these questions, then this book is **not** for you:

1. Can you already create 2D puzzle games?

2. Are you looking for a reference book on Unity programming?

3. Are you an experienced (or at least advanced) Unity user?

If you can answer yes to all four questions, you may instead look for the other books in the series (e.g., 2D platformers or 2D shooters) on the <u>official website</u> (http://www.learntocreategames.com).

HOW YOU WILL LEARN FROM THIS BOOK

Because all students learn differently and have different expectations of a course, this book is designed to ensure that all readers find a learning mode that suits them. Therefore, it includes the following:

- A list of the learning objectives at the start of each chapter so that readers have a snapshot of the skills that will be covered.

- Each section includes an overview of the activities covered.

- Many of the activities are step-by-step, and learners are also given the opportunity to engage in deeper learning and problem-solving skills through the challenges offered at the end of each chapter.

- Each chapter ends-up with a quiz and challenges through which you can put your skills (and knowledge acquired) to the test, and see how much you know. Challenges consist in coding, debugging, or creating new features based on the knowledge that you have acquired in the chapter.

- The book focuses on the core skills that you need; some sections also go into more detail; however, once concepts have been explained, links are provided to additional resources, where necessary.

- The code is introduced progressively and is explained in detail.

- You also gain access to several videos that help you along the way, especially for the most challenging topics.

FORMAT OF EACH CHAPTER AND WRITING CONVENTIONS

Throughout this book, and to make reading and learning easier, text formatting and icons will be used to highlight parts of the information provided and to make it more readable.

The full solution for the project presented in this book is available for download on the official website (http://learntocreategames.com/books/).

SPECIAL NOTES

Each chapter includes resource sections, so that you can further your understanding and mastery of Unity; these include:

- A quiz for each chapter: these quizzes usually include 10 questions that test your knowledge of the topics covered throughout the chapter. The solutions are provided on the companion website.

- A checklist: it consists of between 5 and 10 key concepts and skills that you need to be comfortable with before progressing to the next chapter.

- Challenges: each chapter includes a challenge section where you are asked to combine your skills to solve a particular problem.

Author's notes appear as described below:

Author's suggestions appear in this box.

Code appears as described below:

```
public int score;
public string playersName = "Sam";
```

Checklists that include the important points covered in the chapter appear as described below:

- Item1 for check list

- Item2 for check list

- Item3 for check list

HOW CAN YOU LEARN BEST FROM THIS BOOK?

- **Talk to your friends about what you are doing.**

  We often think that we understand a topic until we have to explain it to friends and answer their questions. By explaining your different projects, what you just learned will become clearer to you.

- **Do the exercises.**

  All chapters include exercises that will help you to learn by doing. In other words, by completing these exercises, you will be able to better understand the topic and gain practical skills (i.e., rather than just reading).

- **Don't be afraid of making mistakes.**

  I usually tell my students that making mistakes is part of the learning process; the more mistakes you make and the more opportunities you have for learning. At the start, you may find the errors disconcerting, or that the engine does not work as expected until you understand what went wrong.

- **Export your games early.**

  It is always great to build and export your first game. Even if it is rather simple, it is always good to see it in a browser and to be able to share it with you friends.

- **Learn in chunks.**

  It may be disconcerting to go through five or six chapters straight, as it may lower your motivation. Instead, give yourself enough time to learn, go at your own pace, and learn in small units (e.g., between 15 and 20 minutes per day). This will do at least two things for you: it will give your brain the time to "digest" the information that you have just learned, so that you can start fresh the following day. It will also make sure that you don't "burn-out" and that you keep your motivation levels high.

FEEDBACK

While I have done everything possible to produce a book of high quality and value, I always appreciate feedback from readers so that the book can be improved accordingly. If you would like to give feedback, you can email me at learntocreategames@gmail.com.

DOWNLOADING THE SOLUTIONS FOR THE BOOK

You can download the solutions for this book after creating a free online account at http://learntocreategames.com/books/. Once you have registered, a link to the files will be sent to you automatically.

IMPROVING THE BOOK

Although great care was taken in checking the content of this book, I am human, and some errors could remain in the book. As a result, it would be great if you could let me know of any issue or error you may have come across in this book, so that it can be solved and the book updated accordingly. To report an error, you can email me (learntocreategames@gmail.com) with the following information:

- Name of the book.

- The page or section where the error was detected.

- Describe the error and also what you think the correction should be.

Once your email is received, the error will be checked, and, in the case of a valid error, it will be corrected and the book page will be updated to reflect the changes accordingly.

SUPPORTING THE AUTHOR

A lot of work has gone into this book and it is the fruit of long hours of preparation, brainstorming, and finally writing. As a result, I would ask that you do not distribute any illegal copies of this book.

This means that if a friend wants a copy of this book, s/he will have to buy it through the official channels (i.e., through Amazon, lulu.com, or the book's official website: www.learntocreategames.com/books).

If some of your friends are interested in the book, you can refer them to the book's official website (http://www.learntocreategames.com/books) where they can either buy the book, enter a monthly draw to be in for a chance of receiving a free copy of the book, or to be notified of future promotional offers.

1
CREATING A WORD GUESSING GAME

In this section, we will start by creating a word guessing game with the following features:

- A word will be picked at random from an existing list.

- The letters of the word will be hidden.

- The players will try to guess each letter by pressing a letter on their keyboard.

- Once a letter has been discovered, it will then be displayed onscreen.

- The player has a limited number of attempts to guess the word.

So, after completing this chapter, you will be able to:

- Read words from a text file.

- Pick a random word.

- Process and assess the letters pressed by the player.

- Display the letters that were correctly guessed by the player.

- Track and display the score.

- Check when the player has used too many guesses.

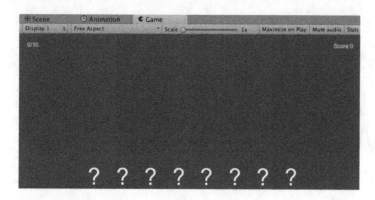

Figure 1: The final game

CREATING THE INTERFACE FOR THE GAME

So, in this section, we will start to create the core of the word guessing game; it will consist of text fields initially blank, and located in the middle of the screen.

So, let's get started:

- Please launch Unity and create a new **Project** (**File | New Project**).

Figure 2: Creating a new project

- In the new window, you can specify the name of your project, its location, as well as the **2D** mode (as this game will be in **2D**).

Figure 3: Specifying the name and location for your project

- Once this is done, you can click on the button called **Create project** (located at the bottom of the window) and a new project should open.

- Once this is done, you can check that the 2D mode is activated, based on the 2D logo located in the top right-corner of the **Scene** view, as illustrated in the next figure.

Figure 4: Activating the 2D mode

First, we will remove the background image for our **Scene**. If you look at your **Game** view, it may look like the following figure.

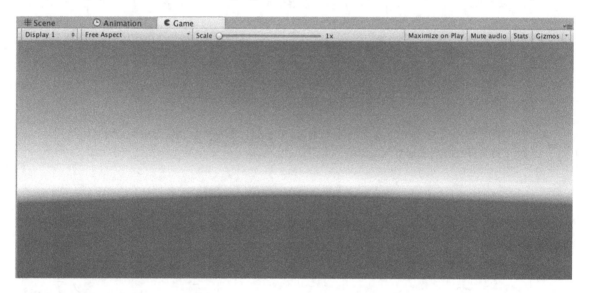

Figure 5: The initial background

If it is the case, then please do the following:

- From the top menu, select: **Window | Lighting**.

- Then delete the **Default Skybox** that is set for the attribute called **SkyBox** (i.e., click on the attribute to the right of the label **Skybox** and press **DELETE** on your keyboard).

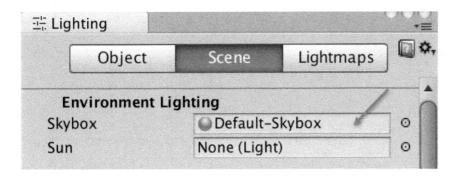

Figure 6: Lighting properties

- Once this is done, your **Game** view should look like the following.

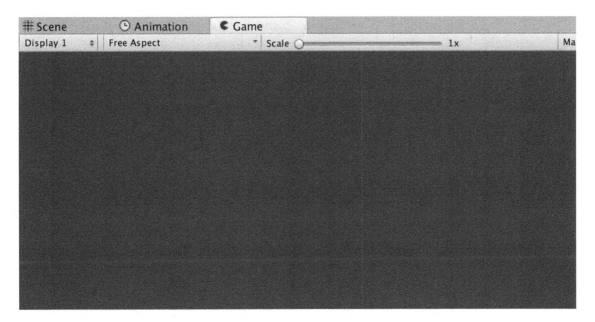

Figure 7: The Game view after deleting the SkyBox

We will now create a text field that will be used for the letters to be guessed.

- From the top menu, please select **GameObject | UI | Text**. This will create a **UI Text** object called **text**, along with a **Canvas** object.

- Please rename this text object **letter**.

Figure 8: Creating a new letter

Select this object (i.e., letter) in the **Hierarchy**, and, using the **Inspector** window, please set its attributes as follows:

- For the component **Rect Transform**: **Position = (0,0,0)**; **Width = 100** and **Height = 100**.

- For the component **Text**: **Font-size = 80**; **Color = white**; **please empty the text**.

- For the component **Text**: **vertical alignment = center**; **horizontal alignment = middle**.

Once this is done, we will create a prefab from this object, so that we can instantiate it later on (i.e., create objects based on this prefab).

- Please drag and drop the object **letter** from the **Hierarchy** window to the **Project** window.

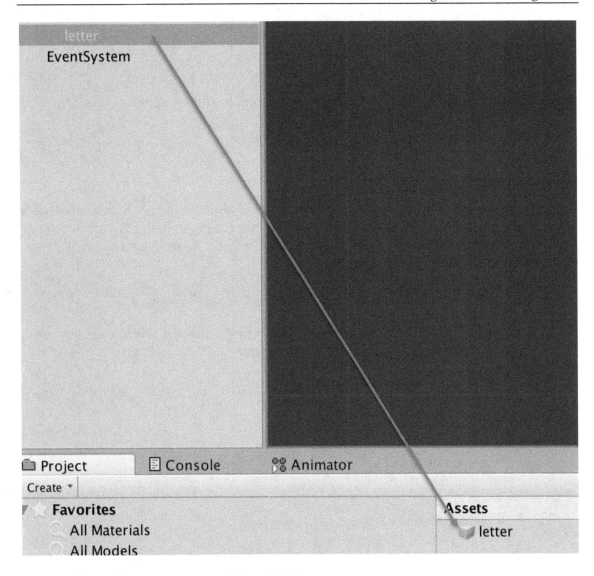

- This will create a new prefab called **letter**.

Next, we will create a **gameManager** object; this object will be in charge of setting the layout for the game and processing the user's entries; in other words, it will be responsible for running and managing the game.

- Please create a new empty object (**GameObject | Create Empty**).

- Rename this new object **gameManager**.

Next, we will create a script that will be attached to the **gameManager** object; this script will be in charge of running the game (e.g., displaying letters, processing user inputs, etc.).

- From the **Project** window, select **Create | C# Script**.

- Rename the new script **GameManager**.

- You can then open this script.

In this script, we will display several letters in the middle of the screen.

- Please add this code at the beginning of the class.

```
public GameObject letter;
```

In the previous code we create a new **public** variable called **letter**; it will be accessible from the **Inspector** since it is public, and it will be set (or initialized) with the **letter** prefab that we have created earlier. This variable will be used to generate new letters based on that template (i.e., the prefab).

- Please check that the code is error free in the **Console** window.

- Drag and drop the script **GameManager** from the **Project** window on the object called **gameManager** located in the **Hierarchy**.

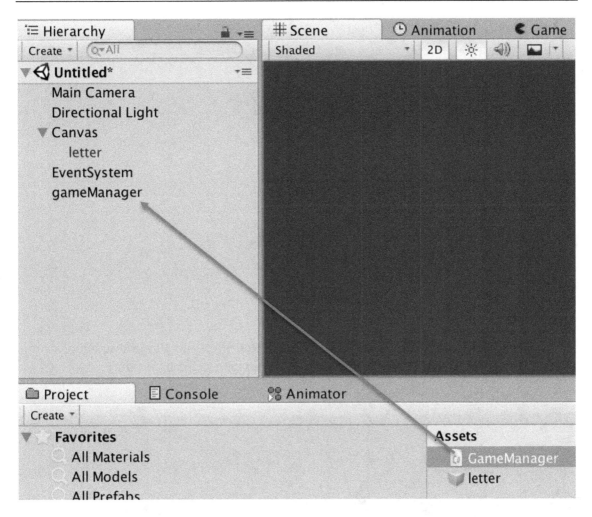

Figure 9: Adding a script to the game manager

- Once this is done, you can select the object called **gameManager** in the **Hierarchy**.

- Using the **Inspector** window, you will see that this object now includes a new component called **GameManager** with an empty field called **letter**.

Figure 10: A new component added to the game manager

- Please drag and drop the prefab called **letter** from the **Project** window to this empty field in the **Inspector** window, as described in the next figure.

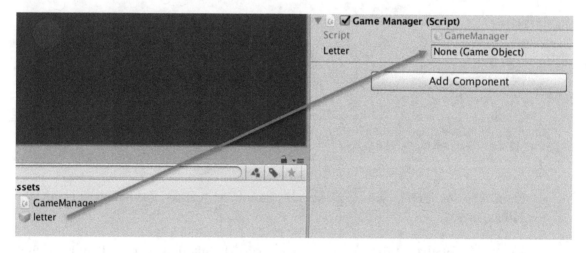

Figure 11: Initializing the letter variable with a prefab

Once this is done, we can start to write a function that will create the new letters.

- Please open the script **GameManager**.

- Add the following code at the end of the class (i.e., just after the function **Update**).

```
void initLetters()
{
    int nbletters = 5;
    for (int i = 0; i < nbletters; i++) {
        Vector3 newPosition;
        newPosition = new Vector3 (transform.position.x + (i *
100), transform.position.y, transform.position.z);
        GameObject l = (GameObject)Instantiate (letter,
newPosition, Quaternion.identity);
        l.name = "letter" + (i + 1);
        l.transform.SetParent(GameObject.Find
("Canvas").transform);

    }
}
```

In the previous code:

- We define that we will display five letters using the variable **nbLetters**; this number is arbitrary, for the time being, so that we can ensure that we can display letters onscreen; this number of letters will, of course, vary later on, based on the length of the word to be guessed.

- We then create a loop that will loop five times (once for each letter).

- In each iteration, we define the position of the new letter using the variable **newPosition**.

- This position of the letter is calculated by combining the position of the object **gameManager** that is linked to this script (i.e., **transform.position**) plus the size of the letter (i.e., **100**; this size/width was set-up earlier-on with the **Inspector** using the **width** attribute) multiplied by the variable **i**; so the position of the first letter on the x-axis will be **transform.position + 0**, the second one will be at the x position **transform.position + 100**, and so on.

- We instantiate a letter and also set its name.

- Finally, we set the parent of this new object to be the object called **Canvas**; this is because, as a **UI Text** object, this object needs to be associated to a canvas in order to be displayed onscreen; this is usually done by default as you create a new **UI Text** object with the editor in Unity; however, this needs to be done manually here, as this object is created and added to the **Scene** from a script.

Finally, please add the following code to the **Start** function.

```
initLetters();
```

As you play the **Scene**, you should see that new letters have been created in the **Hierarchy**.

letter1
letter2
letter3
letter4
letter5

Figure 12: The newly-created letters

If you double-click on one of them (e.g., **letter1**) in the **Hierarchy**, you should see where they are located and their layout in the **Scene** view.

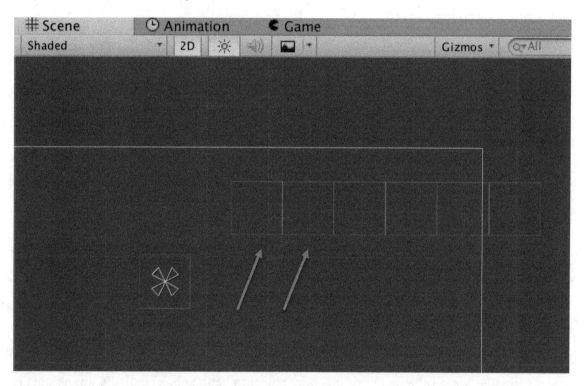

Figure 13: The layout of the letters

Now, because the position of the letters is based on the position of the game manager, you may notice, as for the previous figure, that the letters are not centered properly. So we need to ensure that these letters are properly aligned vertically and horizontally. For this purpose, we will do the following:

- Create an empty text object located in the middle of the screen.

- Base the position of each letter on this object.

- Ensure that all letters are now properly aligned.

So let's proceed:

- Please create a new **UI Text** object (**GameObject | UI | Text**) and rename it **centerOfScreen**.

- Select this object in the **Hierarchy**.

- Using the **Inspector**, in the component called **RectTransform**, change its position to **PosX=0** and **PosY=0**; you can leave the other attributes as they are.

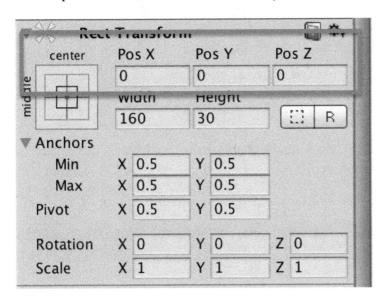

Figure 14: Changing the position attributes

Because this object is a **UI** object, setting its position to (0,0) will guarantee that it will be displayed in the center of the screen; this is because the coordinates of the UI object (for the component **RectTransform**) are based on the view/camera. So **PosX=0** and **PosY=0**, in this case, corresponds to the center of the screen; using an empty object would have been different as the coordinates would be world coordinates and not related to the screen/view.

- Using the **Inspector**, in the component called **Text,** delete the default text, so that this **UI Text** is effectively an empty field.

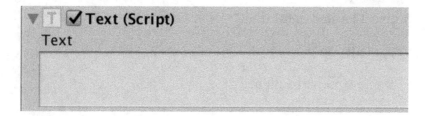

Once this is done, we can modify the code in the script **GameManager** to center our letters.

- Please open the script **GameManager**.

- Add the following code to the start of the class (new code in bold).

```
public GameObject letter;
public GameObject cen;

void Start () {
    cen = GameObject.Find ("centerOfScreen");
    initLetters ();
}
```

- In the previous code, we declare a new variable called **cen** that will be used to refer to the object **centerOfScreen**.

- In the function **initLetter** that we have created earlier-on, please modify this line

```
newPosition = new Vector3 (transform.position.x + (i * 100),
transform.position.y, transform.position.z);
```

… with this code…

```
newPosition = new Vector3 (cen.transform.position.x + (i * 100),
cen.transform.position.y, cen.transform.position.z);
```

In the previous code, we now base the position of our letter on the center of the screen.

- Please save your script, and check that it is error-free.

- Play the **Scene**, and you should see, in the **Scene** view, that the letters are now aligned vertically; however, they are slightly offset horizontally, as illustrated in the next figure.

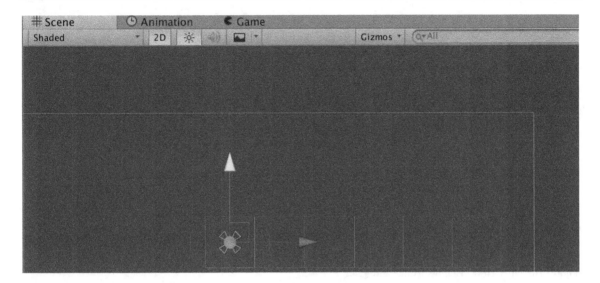

Figure 15: Aligning the letters

So there is a last change that we can include in our script, so that each letter is centered around the center of the screen; this will consist in offsetting the position of each letter based on the center of the screen as follows, so that the middle of the word matches with the center of the screen.

- Please open the script **GameManager** and, in the function called **initLetter**, replace this line:

```
newPosition = new Vector3 (cen.transform.position.x + (i * 100),
cen.transform.position.y, cen.transform.position.z);
```

with this line...

```
newPosition = new Vector3 (cen.transform.position.x + ((i-
nbletters/2.0f)         *100),          cen.transform.position.y,
cen.transform.position.z);
```

In the previous code, we offset the position of each letter based on the center of the screen; so the x-coordinate of the first letter will be **-250**, the x-coordinate of the second letter will be **-150**, and so on.

You can save your script, play the **Scene**, and look at the **Scene** view; you should see that the letters are now properly aligned, as illustrated on the next figure.

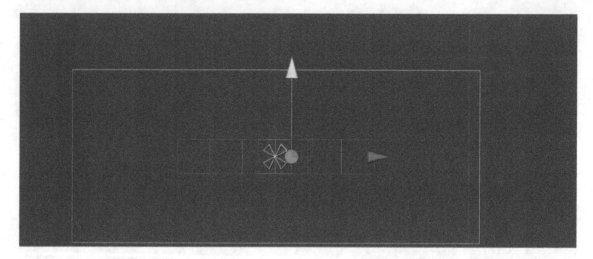

Figure 16: The letters are now properly aligned

If you would like to see what the letters would look like, you can, while the game is playing, select each newly-created letter in the **Hierarchy** and modify its **Text** attribute in the **Inspector** (using the component **Text**), as illustrated in the next figure.

Figure 17: Changing the text of each letter at run-time

DETECTING AND PROCESSING THE USER INPUT

Perfect. So at this stage, we have a basic interface for our game, and we can display letters onscreen. So, in this section, we will implement the main features of the game, that is:

- Create a new word to be guessed.

- Count the number of letters in this word.

- Display corresponding empty text fields.

- Wait for the user to press a key (i.e., a letter) on the keyboard.

- Detect the key pressed by the user.

- Display the corresponding letters in the word to be guessed onscreen.

So let's start.

- Please open the script called **GameManager**.

- Add the following code at the start of the class (new code in bold).

```
public GameObject letter;
public GameObject cen;

private string wordToGuess = "";
private int lengthOfWordToGuess;
char [] lettersToGuess;
bool [] lettersGuessed;
```

In the previous code:

- We declare four new variables.

- **wordToGuess** will be used to store the word to be guessed.

- **lengthOfWordToBeGuessed** will store the number of letters in this word.

- **lettersToGuess** is an array of **char** (i.e., characters) including every single letter from the word to be discovered by the player.

- **letterGuessed** is an array of Boolean variables used to determine which of the letters in the word to guess were actually guessed correctly by the player.

Next, we will create a function that will be used to initialize the game.

- Please add the following function to the class.

```
void initGame()
{
    wordToGuess = "Elephant";
    lengthOfWordToGuess = wordToGuess.Length;
    wordToGuess = wordToGuess.ToUpper ();
    lettersToGuess = new char[lengthOfWordToGuess];
    lettersGuessed = new bool [lengthOfWordToGuess];
    lettersToGuess = wordToGuess.ToCharArray ();
}
```

In the previous code:

- We declare a function called **initGame**.

- In this function, we initialize the variable **wordToGuess**; this will be the word **Elephant** for the time being.

- We then capitalize all the letters in this word; as we will see later in this chapter, this will make it easier to match the letter typed by the user (which usually is upper-case) and the letters in the word to guess.

- We then initialize the array called **lettersToGuess** and **lettersGuessed**.

> Note that for Boolean variables, the default value, if they have not been initialized, is **false**. As a result, all variables in the array called **lettersGuessed** will initially be set to false (by default).

- Finally, we initialize the array called **lettersToGuess** so that each character within corresponds to the letters in the word to guess; for this, we convert the word to guess to an array of characters, which is then saved into the array called **lettersToGuess**.

Once this function has been created, we will need to process the user's input; for this purpose, we will create a function that will do the following:

- Detect the letter that was pressed by the player on the keyboard.

- Check if this letter is part of the word to guess.

- In this case, check if this letter has **<u>not</u>** already been guessed by the player.

- In this case, display the corresponding letter onscreen.

Let's write the corresponding code.

- Please add the following function to the script **GameManager**:

```
void checkKeyboard()
{
    if (Input.GetKeyDown(KeyCode.A))
    {
        for (int i=0; i < lengthOfWordToGuess; i++)
        {
            if (!lettersGuessed [i])
            {
                if (lettersToGuess [i] == 'A')
                {
                    lettersGuessed [i] = true;

    GameObject.Find("letter"+(i+1)).GetComponent<Text>().text   =
"A";
                }
            }
        }
    }
}
```

In the previous code:

- We declare the function called **checkKeyBoard**.

- We then create a loop that goes through all the letters of the word to be guessed; this is done from the first letter (i.e., at the index 0) to the last one.

- We check if this letter has already been guessed.

- If it is **not** the case, we check whether this letter is **A**.

- If this is the case, we then indicate that this letter (i.e., the letter **A**) was found.

- We then display the corresponding letter onscreen.

Last but not least, we just need to be able to call these two functions to initialize the game and to also process the user's inputs.

- Please add the following code to the **Start** function (new code in bold).

```
void Start () {
    cen = GameObject.Find ("centerOfScreen");
    initGame ();
    initLetters ();
}
```

Please make sure that the function **initGame** is called before **initLetters** (as illustrated in the previous code) in the **Start** function; this is because, as we will see later, the function **initLetters** will use some of the information that has been set in the function **initGame** (i.e., the number of letters). So in order for our game to work correctly, the function **initGame** should be called before the function **initLetters**.

- Please add the following code to the **Update** function.

```
void Update () {
    checkKeyboard ();
}
```

The last change we need to add now is linked to the number of letters to be displayed; as it is, the number is set to 5 by default; however, we need to change this in the function called **initLetters**, so that the number of **UI Text** objects that corresponds to the letters in the word to be guessed reflects the length of the word that we have just created.

- Please modify the function **initLetters** as follows (new code in bold).

```
void initLetters()
{
    int nbletters = lengthOfWordToGuess;
```

So at this stage, we have all the necessary functions to start our game; so you can save the script, check that it is error free and play the **Scene**. As you play the **Scene**, if you press the **A** key on the keyboard, the letter **A** should also be displayed onscreen, as it is part of the word **Elephant**.

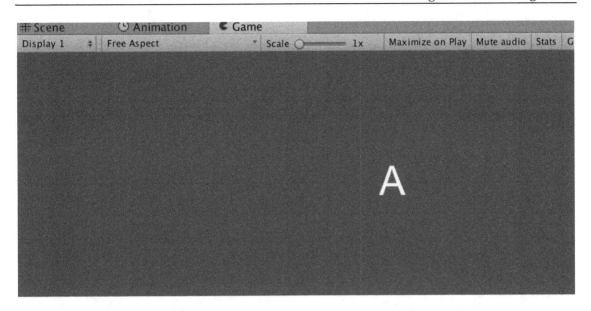

Figure 18: Detecting the key pressed

So, this is working properly, and we could easily add more code to detect the other keys; this would involve using the code included in the function **checkKeyboard**, and copying/pasting it 25 times to be able to detect the other 25 keys/letters, using the syntax **Input.GetKeyDown**, once for each key. So the code could look as follows:

```
if (Input.GetKeyDown(KeyCode.A))
{
...
}
if (Input.GetKeyDown(KeyCode.B))
{
...
}


if (Input.GetKeyDown(KeyCode.Z))
{
...
}
```

Now, this would be working perfectly, however, this would also involve a lot of repetitions (copying 24 times the same code); so to make the code more efficient, we will use a slightly different way of detecting the key pressed by the player. This method will involve the following:

- Check if a key was pressed.

- Check if this key is a letter.

- Proceed as previously to check whether this letter is part of the word to be guessed.

Please create a new function called **checkKeyBoard2**, as follows:

```
void checkKeyboard2()
{
    if (Input.anyKeyDown)
    {
        char letterPressed = Input.inputString.ToCharArray ()
[0];
        int   letterPressedAsInt   =   System.Convert.ToInt32
(letterPressed);
        if (letterPressedAsInt >= 97 && letterPressed <= 122)
        {
            for (int i=0; i < lengthOfWordToGuess; i++)
            {
                if (!lettersGuessed [i])
                {
                    letterPressed   =   System.Char.ToUpper
(letterPressed);
                    if       (lettersToGuess       [i]       ==
letterPressed)
                    {
                        lettersGuessed [i] = true;

    GameObject.Find("letter"+(i+1)).GetComponent<Text>().text   =
letterPressed.ToString();
                    }
                }
            }
        }
    }
}
```

In the previous code:

- We detect whether a key has been pressed using the keyword **Input.anyKeyDown**.

- If this is the case, we save the key (i.e., the letter) that was pressed into the variable called **letterPressed**. For this, given that any key pressed on the keyboard is stored as a string, we need to convert this string value to a character; the character recorded in the variable **letterPressed** will effectively be the first character of the string that corresponds to the key pressed by the player.

- Once this is done, we convert the letter pressed (i.e., character) to an integer value.

- We then check, using the integer value associated with the key pressed, that the key is a letter; this corresponds to an integer value between **97** and **122**.

- Once this final check is complete, we do the exact same as we have done earlier in the function **checkBoard** that we have created previously (i.e., this is the same code).

The last thing we need to do is to call the function **chekBoard2** instead of the function **checkBoard** by amending the **Update** function as follows (new code in bold):

```
void Update () {

    //checkKeyboard ();
    checkKeyboard2 ();

}
```

That's it!

Once this is done, please save your code, check that it is error-free and test the **Scene**. As you press the keys **E, L, P** and **A**, you should see that they now appear onscreen.

Figure 19: Detecting all the keys pressed

CHOOSING RANDOM WORDS

At this stage, the game works properly and the letters that the player has guessed are displayed onscreen; this being said, it would be great to add more challenge by selecting the word to guess at random from a list of pre-defined words. So in the next section, we will learn to do just that; we will start by choosing a word from an array, and then from a text file that you will be able to update yourself without any additional coding.

So let's get started.

- Please open the script **GameManager**.

- Add the following code at the beginning of the class.

```
private string [] wordsToGuess = new string [] {"car",
"elephant","autocar" };
```

- In the previous code, we declare an array of string variables and we add three words to it.

- Add the following code to the function **initGame** (new code in bold).

```
//wordToGuess = "Elephant";
int randomNumber = Random.Range (0, wordsToGuess.Length);
wordToGuess = wordsToGuess [randomNumber];
```

In the previous code:

- We comment the previous code.

- We create a random number that will range from **0** to the **length of the array**. So in our case, because we have three elements in this array, this random number will range from 0 to 2 (i.e., from **0** to **2**).

- We then set the variable called **wordToGuess** to one of the words included in the array called **wordsToGuess**; this word will be picked at random based on the variable called **randomNumber**.

You can now save you script, and check that it is error-free.

There is a last thing that we could do; because the word is chosen at random, the player will not have any idea of the length of this word; so to give an indication of the number of letters to be guessed, we could display questions marks for all the letters to be guessed, onscreen as follows:

- Please select the prefab called **letter** from the **Project** window.

- Using the **Inspector**, and the component called **Text** change its text to **?**, as described in the next figure.

Figure 20: Changing the default charcater for letters

- Lastly, we can also deactivate the object called **letter** that is in the **Hierarchy**.

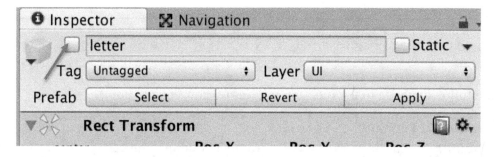

Figure 21: Deactivating the letter object

You can now play the **Scene**, and you should see questions marks where letters need to be guessed.

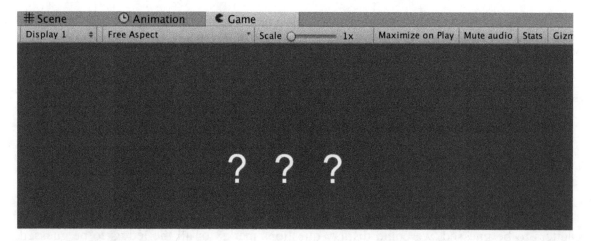

Figure 22: Displaying question marks

TRACKING THE SCORE AND THE NUMBER OF ATTEMPTS

So at this stage, we have a game were we generate random words that need to be guessed by the player. So we will start to finalize our game by adding the following features:

- A starting screen.

- A game-over screen.

- Display the number of guesses.

- Set and display the maximum number of attempts.

- Detect if all the letters in the word to be guessed were found.

- Restart the level with a new word whenever the previous word has been guessed.

- Load the game-over screen if the maximum number of attempts has been reached.

First, we will create s new splash-screen for our game; it will consist of a new **Scene** with a button to proceed to the game. In this splash-screen, we will also initialize the score to 0.

- Please save the current scene as **chapter1**: select **File | Save Scene As...**.

- Create a new scene: from the **Project** view, select **Create | Scene**, and rename it **chapter1_start**.

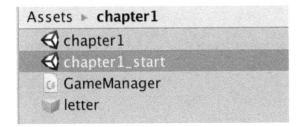

Figure 23: Creating a new Scene

- In the **Project** window, double-click on this new scene.

- If the skybox appears in the background, you can, as we have done in the previous sections, remove it by changing the **Lighting** options (i.e., **Window | Lighting**).

Once this is done, we can create a button that will be used to start the game:

- Please, select **GameObject | UI | Button**; this will create a new button along with its corresponding **Canvas**.

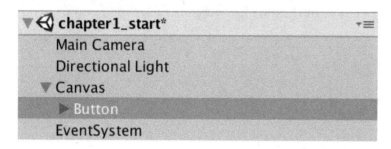

Figure 24: Creating a new button

- Select this button in the **Hierarchy**.

- Using the **Inspector** window, and the component called **RectTransform**, change its position to (**PosX = 0;PosY = 0**).

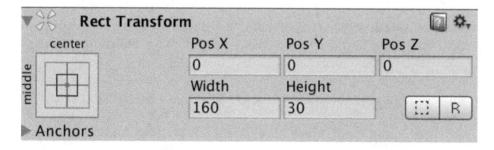

Figure 25: Changing the position of the button

- Using the **Hierarchy**, select the object called **Text** that is a child of the object called **Button,** as illustrated in the next figure.

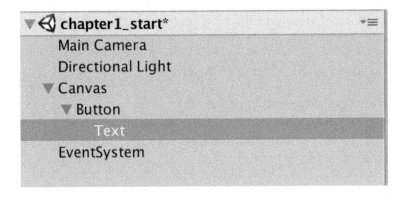

Figure 26: Setting the text for the button

- Using the **Inspector**, in the component called **Text**, change the text attribute to >> Start <<, as described in the next figure.

Figure 27: Changing the text for the button

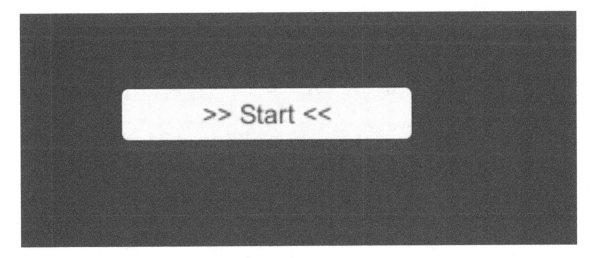

Figure 28: The button with the new text

Next, we need to create a script (and the associated empty object) that will be used to trigger an action when the button is pressed.

- Please create a new empty object (**GameObject | Create Empty**) and rename it **manageButtons**.

- Then, from the **Project** window, select: **Create | C# Script**.

- Rename the new script **ManageButtons** and open it.

We can now add the code that will initialize the score; the new code will also be used to launch the game when the button is pressed.

- Please add the following code at the start of the class (new code in bold):

```
using UnityEngine;
using System.Collections;
using UnityEngine.SceneManagement;
public class ManageButtons : MonoBehaviour {
```

In the previous code we import the library called **SceneManagement**, as we will be using the class **SceneManager** in the next code to load a new **Scene**. The class **SceneManager** is part of the library called **SceneManagement**.

- Please modify the **Start** function as follows:

```
void Start ()
{
    PlayerPrefs.SetInt ("score", 0);
}
```

In the previous code, we declare and initialize a variable called **score**; this variable is saved in the **User Preferences**, which means that it will be accessible throughout the game (i.e., from any scene).

- Please create the following function just before the end of the class:

```
public void startWordGame()
{
    SceneManager.LoadScene ("chapter1");
}
```

In the previous code, we define the function **startWordGame**; when this function is called, the scene called **chapter1** is loaded.

Next, we will link the button to the function **startWordGame**.

- Please save the script and check that it is error-free.

- Once this is done, drag and drop the script **ManageButtons** from the **Project** window to the empty object **manageButton** in the **Hierarchy**, as illustrated in the next figure.

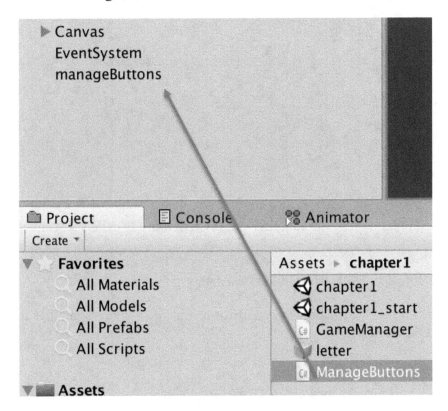

Figure 29: Adding a script to the empty object

You can then select the object **manageButtons** in the **Hierarchy** and look at the **Inspector** window; you should see that the component **ManageButtons** has been added.

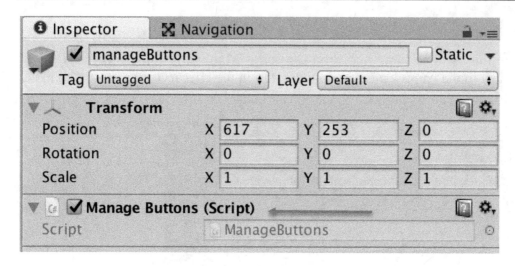

Figure 30: Checking the new component

Next, we will set-up the button so that the function **startWordGame** is called whenever this button is pressed.

- Please select the object called **Button** in the **Hierarchy**.

- Using the **Inspector**, in the section called **Button**, click on the + sign that is below the label **List is Empty**.

Figure 31: Handling clicks (part 1)

Once this is done, this section should now include a new field called **None Object**, as illustrated on the next figure.

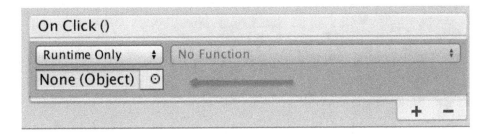

Figure 32: Handling clicks (part 2)

You can then drag and drop the object called **manageButtons** from the **Hierarchy** to the section called **None (Object)** for this object.

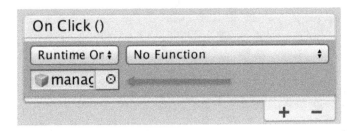

Figure 33: Handling clicks (part 3)

Following this, you can then click on the drop-down menu called "**No Function**" and select: **ManageButtons | startWordGame**. By doing so, we specify that if the button is pressed, the function **startWordGame** from the script **ManageButtons** should be called.

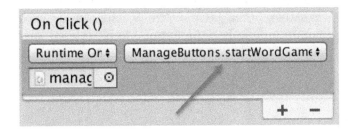

Figure 34: Handling clicks (part 4)

Last but not least, we just need to make sure that all scenes to be played in the game are part of the build settings; this is a way to declare the scenes that should be loaded to Unity.

- Please open the **Build Settings** by selecting **File | Build Settings**.

- Drag and drop the scenes **chapter1** and **chapter1_start** from the **Project** view to the **Build Settings** window.

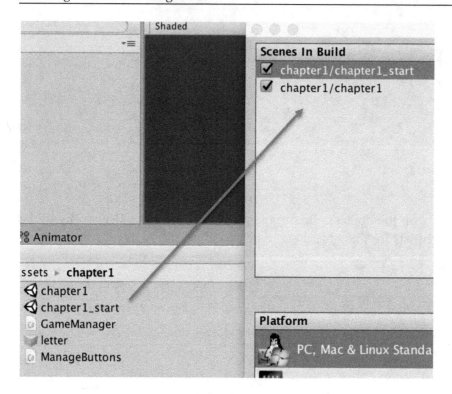

Figure 35: Updating the Build Settings

You can now, play the scene (i.e., **chapter1_start**) and check that the game starts after you press the **START** button.

Next, we will be focusing on recording the number of attempts made by the player. So we will create some code that will track how many guesses the player has made, in the view to evaluate if the player has reached the maximum number of attempts (to be defined later in this section).

- Please save the current scene (**CTRL +S** or **APPLE + S**).

- Open the scene called **chapter1**.

- Open the script called **GameManager**.

- Add the following code at the beginning of the class.

```
private int nbAttempts,maxNbAttempts;
```

- Add the following code to the **Start** function:

```
nbAttempts = 0;
maxNbAttempts = 10;
```

- Please add the following code the function **checkKeyboard2** (new code in bold):

```
if (letterPressedAsInt >= 97 && letterPressed <= 122)
{
        nbAttempts++;updateNbAttempts();
```

In the previous code, we increase the value of the variable **nbAttempts**, and we then refresh the user interface by calling the function **updateNbAttempts**, that we will define in the next paragraph.

- Please create the new function **updateNbAttempts** as follows:

```
void updateNbAttempts()
{
        GameObject.Find ("nbAttempts").GetComponent<Text> ().text =
nbAttempts + "/" + maxNbAttempts;
}
```

In the previous code, we update the text of the **Text UI** object **nbAttempts** (that we have just created) so that it displays the number of attempts made by the player.

- Please add the following line to the **Start** function.

```
updateNbAttempts();
```

- Please save your script, and check that it is error-free.

Finally, we just need to create a **UI Text** object called **nbAttempts** where the number of attempts will be displayed.

- Please create a new **UI Text** component (**GameObject | UI | Text**) and rename it **nbAttempts**.

- Change its **color** to **white**, change its **font-size** to **20**, empty its text, and, using the **Move** tool, place this object in the top-left corner of the white rectangle that defines the viewable area for the player, as described on the next figure.

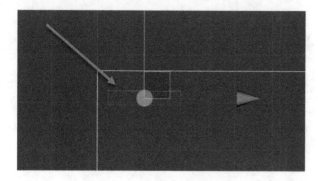

Figure 36: Modifying the user interface

Once this is done, you can test the scene and check that the user interface is updated every time you make a guess (i.e., when you press a letter on the keyboard).

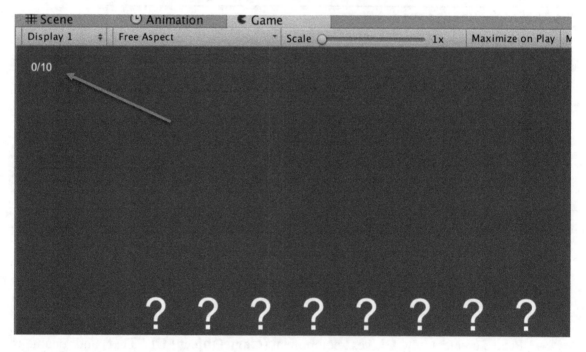

Figure 37: Displaying the number of attempts

Next, we will update the score. So the process will be similar to what we have done previously, as we will:

- Create a **UI Text** object that will display the **score**.

- Increase the **score** whenever a letter has been found.

- Update the text of the corresponding **UI Text** object.

So let's gets started:

- Using the **Hierarchy** window, please duplicate the object called **nbAttempts** and rename the duplicate **scoreUI**.

- Move this object (i.e., **scoreUI**) to the top-right corner of the screen.

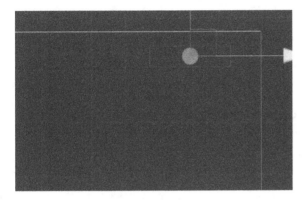

Figure 38: Displaying the score

Once this is done, we can update our script:

- Please open the script called **GameManager**.

- Add this code at the beginning of the class.

```
int score = 0;
```

- Add the following function just before the end of the class (before the last closing curly bracket) so that we can update the score onscreen.

```
void updateScore()
{
    GameObject.Find ("scoreUI").GetComponent<Text> ().text = "Score:"+score;
}
```

- Add the following code to the **Start** function.

```
updateScore()
```

- Modify the function **checkKeyboard2** as follows (new code in bold):

```
if (lettersToGuess [i] == letterPressed)
{
    lettersGuessed [i] = true;
    GameObject.Find("letter"+(i+1)).GetComponent<Text>().text   =
letterPressed.ToString();
    score = PlayerPrefs.GetInt ("score");
    score++;
    PlayerPrefs.SetInt ("score", score);
    updateScore ();
}
```

In the previous code, we just increase the score by one every time the player has guessed a letter correctly; the score accessed from the **Player Preferences**; it is increased by one then saved in the **Player Preferences**, and the interface is then updated accordingly through the function **updateScore**.

- Please save your code, and check that it is error-free. As you play the scene the **score** should be displayed in the top-right corner, as illustrated in the next figure.

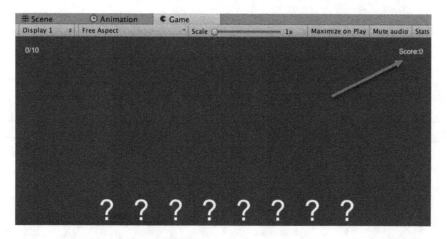

Figure 39: Displaying the score

Now, the last thing we need to do is to check whether the player has guessed the word using less than the maximum number of attempts allowed; if this is the case, a **win** scene will be displayed; otherwise, if the player has failed to guess the word within the maximum number of attempts allowed, a scene called **lose** will be displayed instead. So first, we will create these two scenes (i.e., win and lose).

- Please duplicate the scene called **chapter1_start**: in the **Project** view, select the **Scene** called **chapter1_start**, and press **CTRL + D**.

- This will create a duplicate.

- Please rename the duplicate **chapter1_lose**.

- Open this **Scene** (i.e., **chapter1_lose**).

- Select the object called **Text** in the **Hierarchy**.

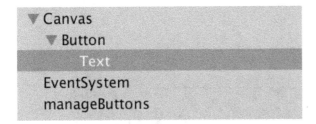

Figure 40: Changing the label of the button

- Using the **Inspector**, for the component called **Text**, change the attribute **text** to >> **RESTART** <<.

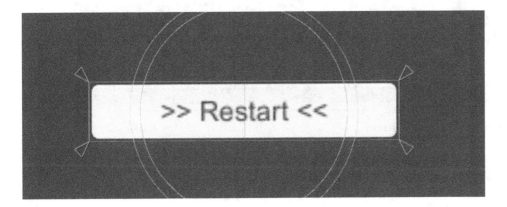

Figure 41:Changing the label of the button

If you wish, you can also add a **UI Text** object with the text "**You Lost**", as follows.

- Create a new **UI Text** object and rename it **message**.

- Using the **Inspector**, change this object's width to **600** and its height to **200**.

- Align its text so that it is centered vertically and horizontally, using the section called **Paragraph** in the component called **Text**.

- Change the font-size to **100**.

- Change the font-color to **white**.

- Center the text both horizontally and vertically.

Please make sure that there is no overlap between the **UI Text** object and the button, otherwise clicks on the button may not be detected.

- Change the text to "**YOU LOST!**".

- The scene should look like the next figure.

Figure 42: Displaying the game-over screen

You can now save the scene.

Last but not least, we will modify the script called **ManageButtons** so that the score is only initialized in the splash-screen.

- Please open the script **ManageButttons**.

- Modify the **Start** function as follows (new code in bold):

```
void Start ()
{
    if (SceneManager.GetActiveScene().name == "chapter1_start")
PlayerPrefs.SetInt ("score", 0);
}
```

In the previous code, the score is initialized only if we are in the scene called **chapter1_start** (i.e., the splash-screen).

Now that the scene called **lose** has been created, we can modify the code used in the game scene so that the **lose** scene is loaded when the number of guesses is more than the maximum allowed.

- Please save the current scene (i.e., press **CTRL + S**).

- Open the scene **chapter1**.

- Open the script called **GameManager**.

- Add the following code at the beginning of the class.

```
using UnityEngine.SceneManagement;
```

- Add the following code to the function **checkKeyboard2** (new code in bold).

```
if (letterPressedAsInt >= 97 && letterPressed <= 122)
{
     nbAttempts++;updateNbAttempts ();
     if (nbAttempts > maxNbAttempts)
     {
          SceneManager.LoadScene ("chapter1_lose");
     }
}
```

In the previous code, we check whether we have reached the maximum number of attempts; in this case, the scene called **chapter1_lose** is loaded.

- Please save your script and check that it is error-free.

We can now add the scene **chapter1_lose** to the **Build Settings** (i.e., select **File | Build Settings**) as we have done for the other scenes.

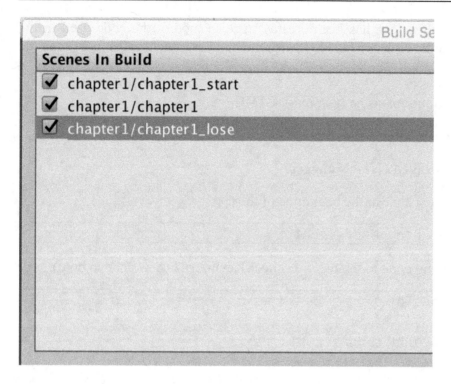

Figure 43: Adding a Scene to the Build Settings

Once this is done, you can play the scene; as you reach the maximum number of attempts, the **lose** scene should be displayed.

Next, we will create code that will assess whether the player has managed to guess all the letters in the word. For this purpose, we will do the following:

- Create a function that will be called whenever the player has correctly guessed a letter.

- This function will check if all the letters were guessed accurately.

- In this case, it will save the word to be guessed, and then display it in the **win** scene.

So let's create this function:

- Please open the script **GameManager**.

- Add the following script at the end of the class.

```
void checkIfWordwasFound()
{
    bool condition = true;
    for (int i = 0; i < lengthOfWordToGuess; i++)
    {
        condition = condition && lettersGuessed [i];
    }
    if (condition)
    {
        PlayerPrefs.SetString                    ("lastWordGuessed",
wordToGuess);
        SceneManager.LoadScene ("chapter1_well_done");
    }
}
```

In the previous code:

- We define a function called **checkIfWordWasFound**.

- We then declare a Boolean variable called **condition** that will be used to
  determine if all the letters were found.

- This variable called **condition** is initially set to true.

- We then go through each variable of the array called **letterGuessed** to check the
  letters that were guessed correctly by the player. If one of the word's letters was
  not found (i.e., even just one), the variable called **condition** will be set to false.

- The following code effectively performs a logical **AND** between all the variables
  of the array **lettersGuessed**, as all of them need to be true (i.e., found) for the
  variable **condition** to be **true**; so this is the same as saying "**if letter1 was
  guessed, and letter2 was guessed and letter3 was guessed, ..., and the last
  letter was guessed then the condition is true**"

```
condition = condition && lettersGuessed [i];
```

- If the variable **condition** is **true**, we then save the word that was guessed in the
  player preferences, so that it can be accessed and displayed in the next scene.

- We then load the **win** scene (that we yet have to create).

We can now add a call to this function from the **checkKeyboard2** function, as follows
(new code in bold):

```
score++;
PlayerPrefs.SetInt ("score", score);
updateScore ();
checkifWordWasFound ();
```

So, we just need to create that new scene:

- Please save your code and check that it is error free.

- Using the **Project** window, duplicate the scene called **chapter1_lose (CTRL + D)** and rename the duplicate **chapter1_well_done**.

- Open the new scene called **chapter1_well_done**.

- Using the **Inspector**, duplicate the object called **Text** (the one used to display the message "**YOU LOST**") and rename the duplicate **wordGuessed**.

- Using the **Move** tool, move the object **wordGuessed** below the button that is already in the scene, as in the next figure.

Figure 44: Moving the new UI Text

- We can change the text of the **UI Text** called **Text**, so that it now displays the text "**YOU WON**".

- We can also empty the text of the **UI Text** object **wordGuessed** so that the interface looks like the next figure.

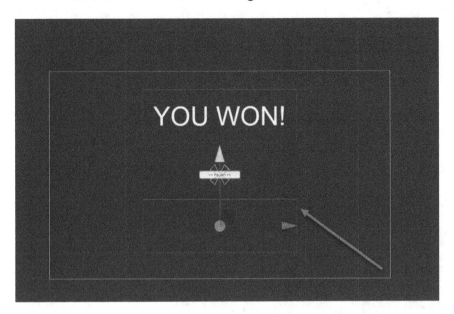

Figure 45: Modifying the GUI

We will now create a script that will be attached to the object **wordGuessed** and that will display the actual word that was just guessed by the player.

- Please create a new C# script called **DisplayLastWordGuessed**.

- Drag and drop this script on the object called **wordGuessed**.

- Open this script.

- Add this code at the beginning of the script.

```
using UnityEngine.UI;
```

- Modify its **Start** function as follows:

```
void Start ()
{
     GetComponent<Text>().text        =        PlayerPrefs.GetString
("lastWordGuessed");
}
```

- Please save your script and your scene.

- Add your scene to the **Build Settings**.

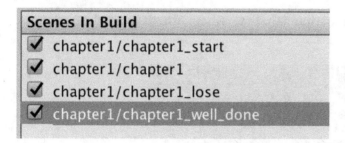

Figure 46: Adding the last Scene to the Build Settings

We can now open the main scene **chapter1**, and test the transition to the **win** scene.

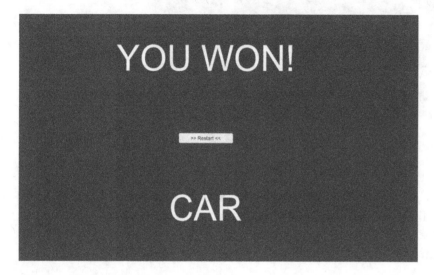

Figure 47: Displaying the win screen

CHOOSING WORDS FROM A FILE

At this stage, the word game is pretty much functional with words selected at random; this being said, the words that we are using are part of an array that we need to update manually; if you were to include 100 words, you would need to enter them manually, which could be time-consuming. So in this section, we will use a technique that consists of selecting a word from a pre-existing list of words saved in a text file. Because such files are available on the Internet, you could virtually create a word guessing game in several languages, by just modifying the file that contains these words.

So we will proceed as follows:

- Import a file with that includes a list of words.

- Add this file to a folder in Unity, where it can be accessed from a script.

- Access this file from our script.

- Pick a random word from this file.

So let's get started.

- Please create a new folder in the **Assets** folder, and call it **Resources**: select the **Assets** folder in the **Project** window, and then select **Create | Folder** from the **Project** window.

- Rename this folder **Resources**.

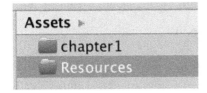

Figure 48: Adding a new folder

- Once this is done, please import the file called **words.txt** from the resource pack that you have downloaded from the companion website to the folder **Resources** that you have just created.

Creating a Word Guessing Game

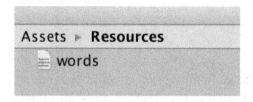

Figure 49: Importing the word file

Next, we will modify our code:

- Please open the script **GameManager**.

- Add the following code just before the end of the class.

```
string pickAWordFromFile()
{
    TextAsset    t1    =    (TextAsset)Resources.Load("words",
typeof(TextAsset));
    string s = t1.text;
    string[] words = s.Split ("\n"[0]);
    int randomWord = Random.Range (0, words.Length + 1);
    return (words[randomWord]);
}
```

In the previous code:

- We create a variable of type **TextAsset** that will point to the text file that we have just imported.

- We then store the text from this file in a variable called **s**.

- Since this file consists of one word per line, we split this string into lines, so that the variable **words** now contains an array of all the words (i.e., lines) included in the file.

Note that the command **string.Split()** will split a string based on a specific character; in our case it is the **end of line** which is symbolized in computer terms by "**\n**".

- The syntax **words = s.Split ("\n"[0]);** means that we split the string called **s** based on the separator "**end of line**" (i.e., \n).

Last but not least, we just need to pick one of these words at random.

- Please modify the function called **initGame** as follows.

[64]

```
//wordToGuess = wordsToGuess [randomNumber];
wordToGuess = pickAWordFromFile ();
```

That's it.

You can now try the game again and check that it works.

There are a few things that you could then modify, for example:

- You could set the number of attempts to the number of letters in the word to be guessed.

- You could also display the word that was to be guessed in the **lose** scene.

- Finally, you could also use sound effects to provide feedback on whether the letter that was selected was correct.

LEVEL ROUNDUP

In this chapter, we have learned to create a simple word guessing game where the player can guess the letters of a particular word. Along the way, we have learned a few interesting skills including: generating random numbers, reading words from a file, using player preferences to save information between scenes, or detecting the player's input. So, we have covered considerable ground to get you started with your first word game!

Checklist

You can consider moving to the next stage if you can do the following:

- Create random numbers.

- Access a text file from a script.

- Update the text of **UI Text** object from a script.

- Create an array of string or Boolean variables.

- Detect the keys pressed by the player.

Quiz

Now, let's check your knowledge! Please answer the following questions (the answers are included in the resource pack) or specify if these statements are either correct or incorrect.

1. The following code will declare an array of integers.

```
int [] i = new int [];
```

2. The following code will declare and initialize an array of string variables:

```
string    []    wordsToGuess    =    new    string    []    {"car",
"elephant","autocar" };
```

3. The following code will check whether the player has pressed the key called A.

```
if (Input.GetKeyDown(A))
```

4. The following code will display the number of characters in the string **Hello**.

```
string s = "Hello";
print(s.Length);
```

5. A **char** variable can be used to store a name with more than two letters.

6. A **string** variable can be used to store a name with more than two letters.

7. The following code will generate a random number between 0 and 100.

```
float randomNumber = Random.Number (0, 100);
```

8. The first element of an array starts at the index 1.

9. The first element of an array starts at the index 0.

10. The following code will store the score in the player preferences:

```
PlayerPrefs.SetInt ("score",score);
```

Challenge 1

Now that you have managed to complete this chapter and that you have created your first level, you could improve it by doing the following:

- Set the number of attempts to the number of letters in the word to be guessed.

- Display the word that was to be guessed in the **lose** scene.

Challenge 2

Another interesting challenge could be as follows:

- Create a text file of your choice with a word on each line.

- Use this word file instead for your game.

2
CREATING A MEMORY GAME

In this section, we will learn how to create a memory game similar to the Simon Game, whereby the player needs to remember a sequence of colors associated to a sound. As the game progresses, the sequence will become longer, hence, increasing the challenge for the player.

After completing this chapter, you will be able to:

- Generate sound effects from Unity and modify their frequency.

- Detect when a player has pressed a button.

- Generate colors at random.

- Generate a sequence of colors and sound.

- Record the sequence entered by the player and compare it to the correct sequence.

INTRODUCTION

In this chapter, we will learn how to create visual and sound effects. We will also create a process by which a sequence of colors is created, and then compared to the sequence entered by the player.

The game will consist of four colored boxes that the player will need to press to reproduce a sequence created randomly by the game.

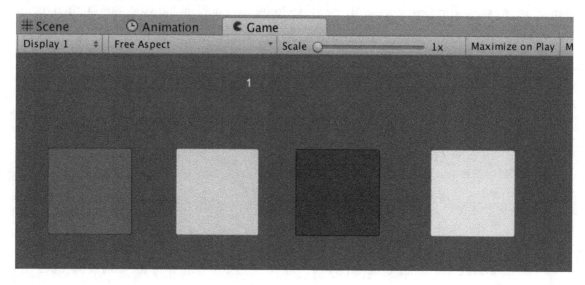

Figure 50: A preview of the game

CREATING THE INTERFACE AND THE CORE OF THE GAME

In this section, we will create the interface for the game; it will consist of four buttons of different colors that the player can click on.

So' let's proceed:

- Please save your current scene (**File | Save Scene**).

- Create a new scene for this new game (**File | New Scene**).

- Rename this new scene **chapter2** (**File | Save Scene As**).

- If the skybox appears by default, you can, as we have done in the previous chapter, remove it using the menu **Window | Lighting**.

Once this is done, we can start to create the buttons that will be used for our game.

- Please create a new button: from the top menu, select **GameObject | UI | Button**. This will create a new object called **Button**, and a parent object called **Canvas**.

- Rename the object called **Button** to **red**.

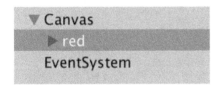

Figure 51: Adding a button

- Please select the object called **red**, and, using the **Inspector**, change its color to **red**, by modifying the **color attribute** of its component called **Image**, as per the next figure.

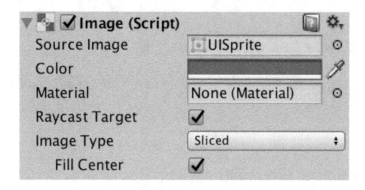

Figure 52: Changing the color of the button

- We can also change its size, so that it looks like a square: please change the **width** and **height** of this object (for the component **Rect Transform**) to **160**.

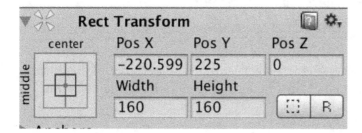

Figure 53: Modifying the size of the button

Last, we will empty the label of this button.

- Using the **Hierarchy**, select the object called **Text** that is a child of the button called **red**.

Figure 54: Emptying the label of the button (part 1)

- Using the **Inspector**, empty the attribute called **text** for its component called **Text**, as per the next figure.

Figure 55: Emptying the label for the button (part 2)

So, at this stage, your button should look like the one illustrated in the next figure.

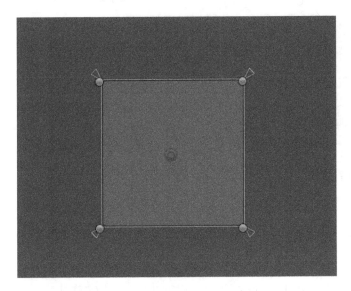

Figure 56: Displaying the red button

So the next step for now is to create the three other buttons by **duplicating** the **red** button:

- Please select the object called **red** in the **Hierarchy** window.

- Duplicate it three times so that you have three duplicates.

- Rename the duplicates **green**, **blue**, and **yellow**.

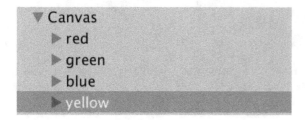

Figure 57: Duplicating the red button

- Using the **Move** tool, move each duplicate apart, as illustrated on the next figure.

Figure 58: Aligning the buttons

- For each of the duplicates: select the corresponding button in the **Hierarchy**, and change its color to **green**, **blue**, and **yellow**, so that the color that you choose matches the name of the corresponding object. You can change the color of a button by selecting this object, and by using the **Inspector** to modify its **Image component**, as described in the next figure.

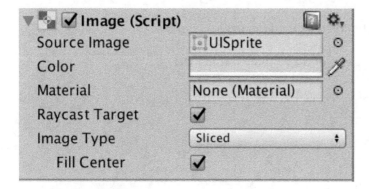

Figure 59: Changing the color of a button

- Once this is done, your **Scene** view may look like the next figure.

Figure 60: Four buttons with colors

DETECTING WHEN BUTTONS HAVE BEEN PRESSED

Next, we will create an empty object and a script that will be used to detect when a button has been pressed.

- Please create an empty object (**GameObject | Create Empty**) and rename it **manageBt**.

- Create a new C# script called **TouchButton**.

- Add this script (i.e., drag and drop it) to the empty object called **manageBt**.

- Select the object called **red** in the **Hierarchy**.

- For this object and in its component called **Button**, click on the + sign located under the label "**List is Empty**", as illustrated in the next figure.

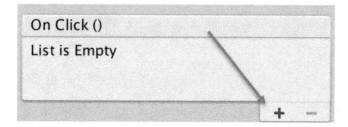

- You can then drag and drop the object called **manageBt** from the **Hierarchy** to the empty field that you have just created, as illustrated on the next figure.

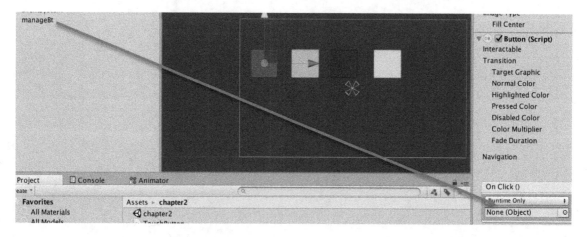

Figure 61: Managing the clicks on buttons (part 1)

- The component called **Button** should then look as illustrated on the next figure.

Figure 62: Managing the clicks on buttons (part 2)

Now, we just need to modify our script **TouchButton**, to create a function that will be called whenever the player clicks on the button.

- Please open the script called **TouchButton**.

- Add the following code at the beginning of the class.

```
using UnityEngine.EventSystems;
```

- This line is necessary, as we will be using some of the classes from the library called **EventSystems** in the next code.

- Add this new function to the script (i.e., just before the last closing curly bracket).

```
public void touchButton()
{
    print        ("You       have       pressed       "      +
EventSystem.current.currentSelectedGameObject.name );
}
```

In the previous code:

- We define a function called **touchButton**.

- When this function is called, it displays the name of the object that is currently selected (i.e., the button that we have clicked);

> We would usually employ the syntax **gameObject.name** to obtain the name of an object linked to a script; however, in this particular case, this script is linked to an empty object (i.e., **manageBt**), so calling **gameObject.name** would return the name of the empty object (i.e., **manageBt**), which is not useful for us, since we want to determine the button that was pressed; so instead, because an event is generated when we click on a button, we use this event to determine the button we have just clicked on; hence the code **EventSystem.current.currentSelectedGameObject.name**.

- Please save your code and check that it is error-free.

The last thing we need to do is to specify that the function called **touchButton** should be called whenever the **red** button is clicked. For this, we will proceed as follows:

- Select the object called **red** in the **Hierarchy**.

- In the **Inspector** window, for the attribute **Button**, locate the section called **On Click**() and select the drop-down menu called **No Function**, as illustrated on the next figure.

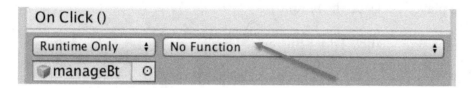

Figure 63: Selecting the function to be called

- Then, from the drop-down menu, select **TouchButton | touchButton** to specify that the function called **touchButton** should be called if we click on this button.

You can now play the scene and check that, after pressing the red button, a message appears in the **Console** window.

So now, we just need to repeat the previous steps for the three other buttons.

To save you time, and instead of repeating the same actions three times, you could proceed as follows:

- Select the three buttons **green**, **blue** and **yellow** in the **Hierarchy** (e.g., left-click + **SHIFT**).

- Because all three objects are selected, the changes that we are about to make will be applied to all three.

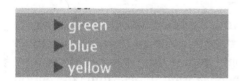

Figure 64: Selecting the three buttons

- In the **Inspector**, in the component called **Button**, click on the + sign located under the label "**List is Empty**", as illustrated in the next figure.

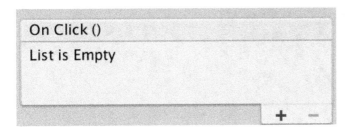

Figure 65: Adding an event

- You can then drag and drop the object called **manageBt** from the **Hierarchy** to the empty field that we just created.

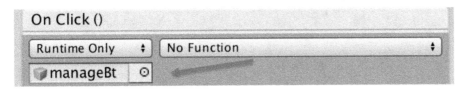

Figure 66: Adding the manageBt object

- Then select **TouchButton | touchButton** to specify that the function called **touchButton** should be called if we click on this button.

Figure 67: Selecting the corresponding function

To check that this has been applied to all three buttons you can just play the scene, press on any of the four buttons, and check that a corresponding message appears in the **Console** window, as illustrated in the next figure.

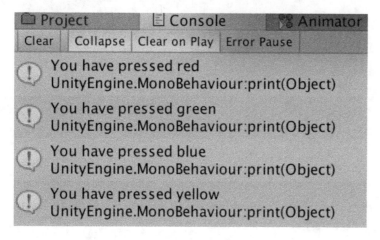

Figure 68: Displaying a message for each button

MANAGING THE GAME

Ok, so at this stage, we have four buttons and we can detect when the player clicks on them. So the next steps will be to:

- Create a **game manager** object.

- This object (and its associated script) will manage different aspects of the game.

- The actions performed by this manager will depend on states that we will define and that will help to know whether we are waiting for a user input, processing the user's input, or just displaying a new sequence of colors.

First, we will give a label to all four buttons, this is so that they can be identified later-on in our scripts.

- Please select the object called **red** in the **Hierarchy**.

- In the **Inspector** window, click on the drop-down menu called **Untagged**, that is located to the right of the label called **Tag**.

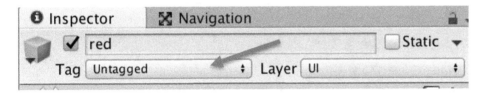

- Select the option **Add Tag** from the drop-down menu.

Figure 69: Selecting a new tag

- In the new window, press three times on the + button that is just below the label "**List is Empty**".

Figure 70: Creating new tags (part 1)

- This will create four placeholders for the new tags that we want to create.

- Create these new tags by entering **1** to the right of the label called **Tag 0**, **2** to the right of the label called **Tag 1**, **3** o the right of the label called **Tag 2**, and **4** to the right of the label called **Tag 3**, as illustrated in the next figure.

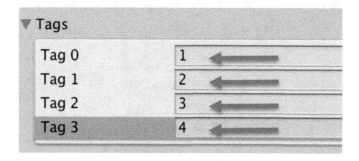

Figure 71: Creating new tags (part 2)

Next, once these tags have been created, we can apply them to the different buttons.

- Please select the button called **red** in the **Hierarchy**.

- Using the **Inspector** window, click to the right of the label called **Tag** and select the tag called **1** from the drop-down menu, as illustrated on the next figure.

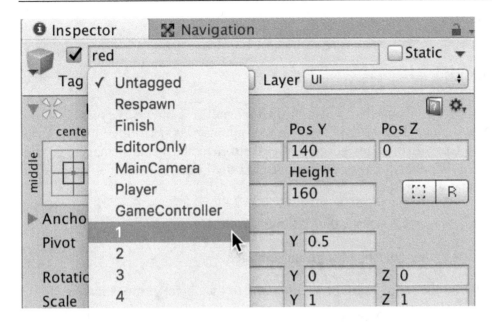

Figure 72: Selecting a tag for each button (part 1)

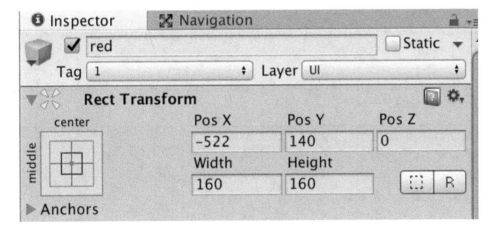

Figure 73: Selecting a tag for the buttons (part2)

Once this is done, you can repeat the last steps to allocate the other tags as follows:

- **Green box**: Tag = 2;

- **Blue box**: Tag = 3;

- **Yellow box**: Tag = 4.

HANDLING CLICKS

Next, we will create a function that will be called whenever a button is pressed. In the previous sections, the handling of the clicks on the buttons was performed by the script **TouchButton**; so we will link this script **TouchButton** to the game manager, so that every time a button is pressed, the game manager is called and receives the name or the tag of the button that was pressed.

- Please create a new C# script called **ManageAudioGame**.

- Create a new empty object called **gameManager**.

- Drag and drop the script **ManageAudioGame** to the object **gameManager**.

- Add the following code at the beginning of the class:

```
int colorSubmitted;
```

In the previous code, we declare the variable **colorSubmitted**, which will store the tag of the button that was just pressed.

- Add the following function just before the end of the class (just before the last closing curly bracket).

```
public void submitColor(int newColor)
{
    print ("You have pressed color " + newColor);
    colorSubmitted = newColor;
}
```

In the previous code:

- We define a function called **submitColor**.

- This function has a parameter called **newColor** that will be used to determine the color of the button that was pressed.

- So when this function is called, it will display the tag number of the button that was just pressed in the **Console** window.

Please save your script.

Next, we just need to be able to call the function **submitColor** every time a button has been pressed, so we will need to modify the script called **TouchButton** accordingly.

- Please open the script **TouchButton**, and modify it as follows (new code in bold).

```
public void touchButton()
{
    //print        ("You        have        pressed        "        +
EventSystem.current.currentSelectedGameObject.name );
    int                        colorNumber                        =
(int)(int.Parse(EventSystem.current.currentSelectedGameObject.tag
));
    GameObject.Find
("gameManager").GetComponent<ManageAudioGame>        ().submitColor
(colorNumber);
}
```

In the previous code:

- We comment the line that displayed the color of the box pressed, as we will display a similar message in the function called **submitColor** in the script **ManageAudioGame**.

- We declare a new variable called **colorNumber**; this number will be set using the tag of the button that was just pressed.

- Because the tag is a **string** value (i.e., text), we use the function **int.Parse** to convert it to an **integer** type.

We also use the expression **(int)** to cast (or convert) it to an **int** type; this is because although we have already converted the **string** to an **int**, Unity needs to ensure that what is on the right side of the equal sign is of the same type as what is on the left side of the equal sign. So by adding a casting in the form of **(int)**, we ensure that values on both sides of the equal sign are of the same type. This is called **casting**.

Before we can test our scene, please ensure that both the scripts **TouchButton** and **ManageAudiogame** are error-free, and also that the script **ManageAudioGame** has been added (i.e., dragged and dropped) to the object **gameManager**.

- You can now test your scene, and press on any of the buttons, and you should see a corresponding message displayed in the **Console** window, as illustrated in the next figure.

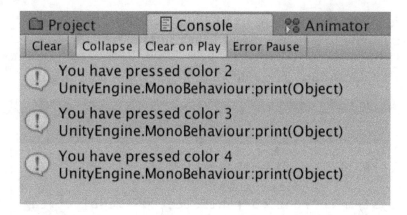

Figure 74: Displaying the tag of the active button

CREATING DIFFERENT STATES FOR OUR GAME

Next, we will declare the different states that will apply to our game.

- Please open the script called **ManageAudioGame**.

- Add the following code at the beginning of the class.

```
private const int STATE_PLAY_SEQUENCE = 1;
private const int STATE_WAIT_FOR_USER_INPUT = 2;
private const int STATE_PROCESS_USER_INPUT = 3;
```

In the previous code:

- We declare three constants; these are variables that will not change throughout our game. Although they are integers, their name will be easier to remember than numbers.

- All these variables are there to define a state in which the game will be at any given time.

So the game will be in one of these states.

- **Playing a sequence of colors**: once a new color has been created, the new sequence that includes all the colors generated is played. Every turn, one new color is added to the sequence.

- **Waiting for the user's input**: After a new sequence has been played/displayed by the game, the player needs to click on the boxes in the correct order to reproduce this sequence.

- **Processing the user's input**: Once the user has pressed the different buttons, the game will need to process this information to determine whether the player has remembered and played the previous sequence correctly.

Once this is done, the game will either add a new color to the sequence, or restart from the beginning.

The core of our game will be based on all these states; so we will now modify the **Update** functions to mirror these different states.

- Please add the following code at the beginning of the class:

```
private int currentState;
```

- Please add the following code in the **Start** function:

```
currentState = STATE_PLAY_SEQUENCE;
```

In the previous code, we just specify that at the start of the game, the game will play the new sequence.

- Please modify the **Update** function as follows:

```
void Update ()
{
    switch (currentState)
    {
        case STATE_PLAY_SEQUENCE:
        break;

        case STATE_WAIT_FOR_USER_INPUT:
        break;

        case STATE_PROCESS_USER_INPUT:
        break;

        default:
        break;
    }
}
```

In the previous code:

- We create a switch statement; this is comparable to branching instructions based on a specific variable; in our case, we will execute code based on the value of the variable called **currentState**.

- So if **currentState** is **STATE_PLAY_SEQUENCE**, we will go to the corresponding section called **STATE_PLAY_SEQUENCE**.

- The idea of this structure is that all branches are mutually exclusive which means that you can be in only one state at any time. So the game will either be playing a new sequence of colors, waiting for the user input, or assessing the user input.

PLAYING A SEQUENCE OF COLORS

Next we will be dealing with the state called **STATE_PLAY_SEQUENCE**; in this state, the game should do the following:

- Pick a color at random.

- Add it to the existing sequence of colors.

- Play the new sequence of colors (including the last color) and light-up the corresponding boxes sequentially.

- Note that if we are at the start of the game, only the new color that has been generated will be displayed (i.e., corresponding boxed lit up).

For this purpose, we will need to do the following:

- Generate a new color at random.

- Store the sequence of colors in an array.

- Hide all the boxes currently displayed onscreen.

- Display (and subsequently hide) each individual box that is part of this sequence.

First, let's create a function that will generate a random number.

- Please add the following code at the beginning of the class:

```
int [] sequenceOfColor = new int[100];
int indexOfColor = 0;
```

In the previous code, we define the array that will be used to store the sequence created by the game.

- Please add the following code to the **Start** function:

```
void Start ()
{

    currentState = STATE_PLAY_SEQUENCE;
    sequenceOfColor = new int[100];
}
```

In the previous code, in addition to specifying the current state, we initialize the array **sequenceOfColor**; as it is, it should handle up to 100 items.

- Please add the following code just before the end of the class:

```
public void generateNewColor()
{

    int r = Random.Range (1, 4);
    sequenceOfColor [indexOfColor] = r;
    indexOfColor++;
}
```

In the previous code:

- We declare a function called **generateColor**.

- We create a new random number with a value that can range between **1** and **4**.

- We then add this number to the array that stores the sequence of colors generated by the game.

- We then increment the index of the array **indexOfColor**. This is so that the next time a color is created, it will be added at the index (or position) **index** in the array.

Next, we will create a function that will hide all the boxes; this is because we want to clear the screen before displaying each of the boxes that are part of the sequence.

- Please add the following code at the beginning of the script **ManageAudioGame** (new code in bold).

```
using UnityEngine;
using System.Collections;
using UnityEngine.UI;
```

In the previous code, we introduce the **UI** library, since will be using some of its element (i.e., **Text**).

- Please add the following code at the end of the class (i.e., before the last closing curly bracket).

```
void hideBoxes()
{
    for (int i = 1; i <= 4; i++)
    {
        GameObject.FindWithTag                (""           +
i).GetComponent<Image>().enabled = false;
    }
}
```

In the previous code:

- We loop through the four boxes that we have created earlier (i.e., the boxes that are onscreen).

- We identify each of these boxes using their tag.

- For each box, we disable the **Image** component, which means that the box will not be visible.

Next, we will need another function that displays a particular box; this is so that we can display individually each of the colors included in the sequence generated by the game.

- Please add the following function at the end of the class **ManageAudioGame** (i.e., just before the last closing curly bracket).

```
public void displayBox(int index)
{
    GameObject.FindWithTag                    (""           +
index).GetComponent<Image>().enabled = true;
}
```

In the previous code:

- We declare a new function called **displayBox**, that will be used to display a particular box.

- We identify a box based on its tag.

- For this particular box, we enable the **Image** component, which means that the box will be visible.

Please save your script. At this stage, you can test the functions **hideBoxes** and **displayBox** by adding the following code to the **Start** function.

```
hideBoxes ();
displayBox (1);
```

- As you play the Scene, you should see that only the red box is displayed.

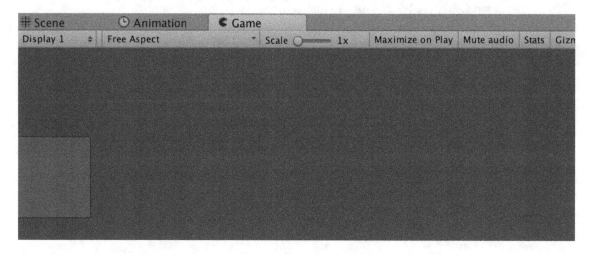

Figure 75: Testing the functions

CREATING A NEW SEQUENCE OF COLORS

Now that we can hide and display boxes, we will get to do the following:

- Pick a color/box at random.

- Add it to a new sequence.

- Display the sequence.

- Make sure that there is a delay between the display of each box, so that the sequence can be identified clearly by the player (i.e., otherwise, the sequence will be displayed too fast to be remembered).

- Wait for the player to reproduce this sequence by clicking on the corresponding boxes.

First, we will create a timer; this timer will be used to display each of the colors that are part of the sequence generated by the game.

- Please add the following code to the beginning of the class:

```
bool          newColorHasBeenGenerated,          allBoxesDisplayed,
startTimer,waitingTimerActivated,waitingTimeElapsed;
float timer, waitingTime, timeDelayBetweenDisplays;
int animationIndex, nbColorsSubmitted;
```

In the previous code, we declare a set of variables that will be used for the state called **STATE_PLAY_SEQUENCE**; each of these variables will be explained in the next sections.

- Please add the following code to the **Start** function:

```
newColorHasBeenGenerated = false;

startTimer = false;
waitingTimerActivated = false;
waitingTimeElapsed = false;
allBoxesDisplayed = false;
timer = 0;
waitingTime = 0;
animationIndex = 0;
timeDelayBetweenDisplays  = 2;
nbColorsSubmitted = 0;
```

In the previous code:

- We set the variable **newColorHasBeenpicked** to false.

- This variable is used to know whether the game has already picked a new color at random.

- We also declare a series of variables that will be explained in details later.

Once this is done, we can look at what the game should do in the state called **STATE_PLAY_SEQUENCE.**

- Please add the following code to the switch section that corresponds to the state **STATE_PLAY_SEQUENCE** (new cod in bold).

```
case STATE_PLAY_SEQUENCE:
if (!newColorHasBeenGenerated) {
    initTimer ();
    generateNewColor ();
    newColorHasBeenGenerated = true;
    allBoxesDisplayed = false;
    hideBoxes ();
}
```

In the previous code:

- We are in the state called **STATE_PLAY_SEQUENCE**, a state where the game is supposed to pick a new colored box at random, add this color to the existing sequence, and then play the full sequence (including the last color picked).

- If a new random color has not yet been picked, we proceed as follows.

- We call a function called **initTimer** that we yet need to define; this function will basically initialize the timer that will be used to make sure that there is enough time or delay between the display of each box in the sequence.

- We call the function **generateNewColor**; if you remember well, this function picks a color at random and adds it to a sequence.

- Next, we specify that we have picked a new color by setting the variable **newColorHasBeenGenerated** to **true**.

- Finally, we hide all the boxes and set the corresponding value of the variable **allBoxesDisplayed** to **false**.

So we can now add the function **initTimer** at the end of the class (i.e., before the last closing curly bracket), as follows:

```
void initTimer()
{
    startTimer = true;
    timer = 0;
    animationIndex = 0;
}
```

In the previous code:

- We set the variable **startTimer** to true, so that the timer can start ticking.

- Its initial value is **0**.

- The animation index is set to **0**; when we successively display a new sequence to the player, we effectively create an animation that includes several stages depending on the box in the sequence that is currently displayed as part of the animation. So we will start with the first element of the animation (i.e., the first box in the sequence).

We can now resume the structure of the state **STATE_PLAY_SEQUENCE**.

- Please add the following to the code that you have already included in the switch portion that corresponds to the state **STATE_PLAY_SEQUENCE**.

```
timer += Time.deltaTime;
if   (startTimer   &&   timer    >=    timeDelayBetweenDisplays   &&
!waitingTimerActivated) {
    timer = 0;
    hideBoxes ();
    displayBox (sequenceOfColor [animationIndex]);
    animationIndex++;
    if (animationIndex >= indexOfColor) {
        startTimer = false;
        animationIndex = 0;
        waitingTimerActivated = true;
    }
}
```

In the previous code:

- We increase the timer by one every seconds.

- This timer is used to determine when we should display the next part of the animation.

- This is the case when the timer has started (**startTimer** is true), and when we have reached the threshold called **timeDelayBetweenDisplays** (i.e., **timer >= timeDelayBetweenDisplays**).

- We also use a variable called **waitingTimerActivated**; this is employed to add a slight delay at the end of the animation; without this delay, the last color would be displayed too briefly; so we create a waiting timer that will be used once we have reached the end of the sequence, hence, in this particular case, we also require **waitingTimerActivated** to be false.

- When these three conditions are fulfilled, we do the following.

- The timer is reset to 0.

- We then hide all the boxes.

- We display the box at the current index (i.e., **animationIndex**) in the sequence.

- We increase the variable **animationIndex** by one.

- If we have reached the end of the animation (i.e., **animationIndex >= indexOfColor**), we reset the timer, as well as the **animationIndex**, and we also specify that we will add a slight delay at the end of the sequence by activating the waiting timer (i.e., **waitingTimerActivated = true**).

- Please add the following to the code that you have already included in the switch portion that corresponds to the state **STATE_PLAY_SEQUENCE**.

```
if (waitingTimerActivated)
{
    waitingTime += Time.deltaTime;
    if (waitingTime >= timeDelayBetweenDisplays)
    {
        waitingTime = 0;
        waitingTimerActivated = false;
        waitingTimeElapsed = true;
    }
}
```

In the previous code:

- This code is used when the waiting timer is activated at the end of the sequence.

- Once it is activated, we just increase its time every second.

- Whenever it has reached a specific threshold (i.e., **waitingTime >= timeDelayBetweenDisplays**) we then reset this timer.

- Then, the variable **waitingTimeActivated** is set to false (since the delay has already been applied).

Please add the following code just after the code that you have typed.

```
if (waitingTimeElapsed)
{
    currentState = STATE_WAIT_FOR_USER_INPUT;
}
```

In the previous code: if we have reached the end of the animation and applied the slight delay at the end (i.e., **waitingTimeElapsed = true**), then we move on to the next state where the user needs to repeat this sequence.

We can also add the code to re-initialize all the variables used in the animation in the **Start** function, as follows.

```
//hideBoxes ();
//displayBox (1);
indexOfColor = 0;
startTimer = false;
waitingTimerActivated = false;
waitingTimeElapsed = false;
allBoxesDisplayed = false;
timer = 0;
waitingTime = 0;
animationIndex = 0;
timeDelayBetweenDisplays  = 2;
newColorHasBeenGenerated = false;

//testing
sequenceOfColor = new int[] { 1, 2, 3, 4 ,2};
indexOfColor = 4;
```

The last part of the code creates a virtual sequence of colors and sets the variable **indexOfColor** to 4 (remember: for an array, the first element starts at the index 0, so here the index of the last element in this array is not 5 but **4**), indicating that the last element of the sequence (or array) is at the index **4**.

You can now save your script and play the scene, you should see that all the boxes disappear and that a sequence of 5 random boxes is displayed onscreen.

WAITING FOR THE USER'S INPUT

So, at this stage we are able to generate a random color and to play a sequence; so the next step will be to wait for the user input; so, in this section, we will write code that will do the following:

- Wait for the user's input.

- Let the player select (i.e., click on) a sequence of boxes.

- Record the boxes that were selected by the player.

- Record the number of boxes selected.

- When the expected number of boxes has been reached (e.g., if the sequence includes two colors, we expect the player to choose two boxes), we will then check if the correct sequence was entered by the player by comparing it to the sequence previously generated by the game.

- In case the sequence entered by the player is correct, the game will restart the process by generating a new color, and add it to the previous sequence.

- In case the sequence entered by the player is incorrect, the game will restart with a sequence of just one color initially.

Please add the following code at the beginning of the class **ManageAudioGame**.

```
int [] sequenceOfColorsSubmitted = new int[100];
```

In the previous code, we declare an array that will be used to store the sequence of colors chosen by the player.

- Please modify the function **SubmitColor** as follows.

```
public void submitColor(int newColor)
{
      print ("You have pressed color " + newColor);
      if (currentState == STATE_WAIT_FOR_USER_INPUT)
      {
          colorSubmitted = newColor;
          sequenceOfColorsSubmitted        [nbColorsSubmitted]     =
newColor;

          nbColorsSubmitted++;
          if (nbColorsSubmitted == (indexOfColor))
          {
               currentState = STATE_PROCESS_USER_INPUT;
          }
      }
}
```

In the previous code.

- We record the color (or corresponding tag) of the box that was just selected by the player.

- We increase the index of the variable called **nbColorsSubmitted**, so that we know how many boxes the player has selected.

- Then, if the player has selected the required number of boxes, we then proceed to the state called **STATE_PROCESS_USER_INPUT**.

We can then make a few more changes.

- Please modify the **Update** function as follows (new code in bold).

```
if (waitingTimeElapsed)
{
      currentState = STATE_WAIT_FOR_USER_INPUT;
      nbColorsSubmitted = 0;
}
```

- Please, also add the following code to the **Update** function (new code in bold):

```
case STATE_WAIT_FOR_USER_INPUT:
if (!allBoxesDisplayed)
{
     setBoxColors ();
     allBoxesDisplayed = true;
}
```

In the previous code:

- We check whether all the boxes are displayed.

- This is because, in the previous state, the colors are displayed one by one; however, now the player needs to be able to choose the correct sequence; therefore, all boxes should now be displayed, so that the player can click on them.

- We call a function called **setBoxColors** that we yet have to define, that will display all the boxes.

Please add the following code to the class:

```
void setBoxColors()
{
     for (int i = 1; i <= 4; i++)
     {
          GameObject.FindWithTag                    (""              +
i).GetComponent<Image>().enabled = true;
     }
}
```

In the previous code, we display all boxes by activating their **Image** component.

PROCESSING THE USER'S INPUT

In this section, we will process the user's input.

- Please modify the **Update** function as follows (new code in bold) in the class **ManageAudioGame**:

```
case STATE_PROCESS_USER_INPUT:
    bool okResult = assessUserMove ();
    if (okResult) {
        animationIndex = 0;
        newColorHasBeenGenerated = false;
        timer = 0;
        waitingTimerActivated = false;
        waitingTimeElapsed = false;
        currentState = STATE_PLAY_SEQUENCE;
    }
    else
    {

        loadLoseLevel ();
    }
```

In the previous code:

- We are in the state where the game is processing the user's inputs.

- We create a Boolean variable that will store the result returned by the function **assessUserMove**; this function, that we yet have to define, will return **true** if the user has entered the correct sequence, and **false** otherwise.

- So if the player has entered the correct sequence (i.e., if **okResult** is true), then the **animationIndex** is set to **0** (so that the animation can start from the first element of the next sequence); we also re-initialize several of the variables linked to the state **STATE_PLAY_SEQUENCE**, including **newColorHasBeenGenerated**, **timer**, **waitingTimerActivated**, **waitingTimeElapsed**, and **currentState**.

- If the sequence is not correct, we then call a function called **loadLoseLevel**, that we yet have to define, and that will load a scene that indicates that the player has lost.

So next, we can start to create the function **assessUserMove**, so that we can check if the player has entered the correct sequence.

- Please add the following function at the end of the class (i.e., before the end of the last curly bracket).

```
public bool assessUserMove()
{
     bool allPerfect = true;
     for (int i = 0; i < indexOfColor; i++) {
          int a = sequenceOfColor [i];
          int b = sequenceOfColorsSubmitted [i];
          if (a != b)
               allPerfect = false;
          //print ("Color1: " + a + "/" + b);
     }
     if (allPerfect)
     {print ("WELL DONE!");return true;}
     else {print ("NOT RIGHT!"); return false;}

}
```

In the previous code:

- We define a Boolean variable called **allPerfect** and set it to true. This variable will be used to determine if all the colors selected by the player were entered in the right sequence; if any error was made, this variable (i.e., **allPerfect**) will be set to false.

- We then loop through the colors entered by the player; the variable **indexOfColor** indicates the number of colors entered by the player; so we go from the first to the last color chosen by the player. The sequence of colors entered by the player is stored in the variable **sequenceOfColorsSubmitted** and the correct sequence of colors is submitted in the array **sequenceOfColor**; so we compare these two arrays at the current index (e.g.., for the first or the second color chosen).

- If the colors are different at the current index, then the variable **allPerfect** is set to false; so at the end of the loop, if one of the colors amongst the sequence chosen by the player is incorrect, the variable **allPerfect** is set to **false** and the value **false** is returned.

- Otherwise, the value **true** is returned.

Last but not least, we will create the function **loadLoseLevel** that will be called when the player has entered the incorrect sequence along with the corresponding scene.

- Please add the following code at the beginning of the class (new code in bold):

```
using UnityEngine;
using UnityEngine.UI;
using System.Collections;
using UnityEngine.SceneManagement;
```

- Please add the following code at the end of the class (i.e., just before the last closing curly bracket).

```
public void loadLoseLevel()
{
        PlayerPrefs.SetInt ("score", indexOfColor-1);
        SceneManager.LoadScene ("chapter2_lose");
}
```

In the previous code:

- We define the function **loadLoseLevel**.

- In this function, we save the score, which is basically the length of the sequence that the player has managed to reproduce. So, for example, if the player has managed to remember a sequence of two colors but has failed to remember (and to reproduce) the next sequence, then the score will be **2**. Because **indexOfColors** is incremented just before we start a new sequence, we need to subtract one from this number to calculate the correct score if the current sequence has not reproduced correctly.

- We then load the scene called **chapter2_lose** (that we yet have to create).

So before we check for incorrect answers, we can just check if the game works for correct inputs.

Please comment the following code in your script:

```
//sequenceOfColor = new int[] { 1, 2, 3, 4 ,2};
//indexOfColor = 4;
```

- Please save your script and check that it is error-free

- You can play the scene.

- The game will display one color, then wait for your input. As you click on the right color, it should now display two colors, and wait for your input again. You should also see the following (or similar) messages in the **Console** window.

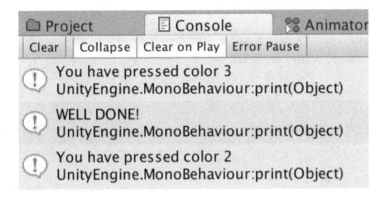

Figure 76: Testing the game

Now that you have checked that the game plays correctly, we can now create the scene called **lose**, so that the game also accounts for incorrect inputs; the new scene will include a text field that will be used to display the score as well as a button that the player will be able to click to restart the game.

- Please save the current scene as **chapter_2_lose** (File | Save Scene As).

- Create a new scene (**File | New Scene**).

- You can, as we have done in the past, remove the skybox from your scene (i.e., **Window | Lighting**).

- Add a **Text UI** object to the **Scene (GameObject | UI | Text)** and rename it **scoreUI**.

- You can center it in the middle of the screen using the **Scene** view or the **Inspector** (i.e., by modifying the attributes **PosX** and **PosY** for the component **Rect Transform**).

- You can also change the **font size** to **20**, and its alignment, as illustrated in the next figure.

Paragraph

Alignment

Figure 77: Changing the alignment of the text

When this is done, we just need to create a script that we will link to this object and that will display the score through the object called **scoreUI**.

- Please create a new C# script and call it **LoseScreen**.

- Add the following code at the beginning of the class (new code in bold).

```
using UnityEngine;
using System.Collections;
using UnityEngine.UI;
```

- Then modify the **Start** function as follows (new code in bold).

```
void Start ()
{
    GameObject.Find  ("scoreUI").GetComponent<Text>  ().text  =
"Score :" + PlayerPrefs.GetInt ("score");
}
```

In the previous code, we display the score using the object **scoreUI**.

- Please save your code and make sure that this script (i.e., **LoseScreen**) is added (or linked) to the object called **scoreUI**.

Next, we just need to create a button that the player can use to reload the main scene and restart the game.

- Please create a new button (i.e., select: **GameObject | UI | Button**).

- Modify the label of this button to >> **Restart** << using the object **Text** that is a child of the object called **Button** in the **Inspector**, as illustrated in the next figure.

Figure 78: Changing the label of the button (part 1)

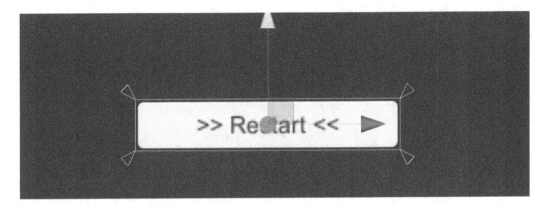

Figure 79: Changing the label of the button (part 2)

Once this is done, we just need to do the following, as we have done previously:

- Create an empty object.

- Create a new script with a function that should be called when the button is pressed.

- Link the button to this script.

So let's proceed:

- Please create a new empty object (**GameObject | Create Empty**) and rename it **manageBt**.

- Create a new script called **ManageBtChapter2**.

- Open this script.

- Add the following code at the beginning of the class (new code in bold).

```
using UnityEngine;
using System.Collections;
using UnityEngine.SceneManagement;
```

- Add the following function to this script.

```
public void restart()
{
    SceneManager.LoadScene ("chapter2");
}
```

Please save your script and drag and drop it to the object **manageBt**.

- Select the object called **Button** in the **Hierarchy**.

- Using the **Inspector**, click on the + button located below the label called **OnClick**.

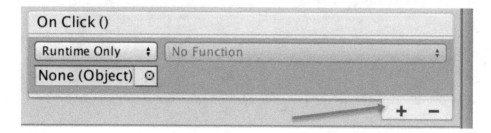

Figure 80: Managing events (part1)

- Drag and drop the object **manageBt** to the empty field called **NoneObject**.

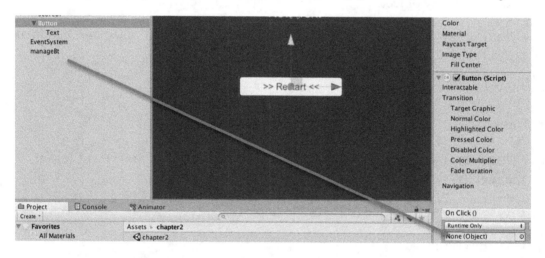

Figure 81: Managing events (part 2)

- And finally, select the option **ManageBtChapter2 | Restart** from the menu to the right of the label **Runtime Only**.

Figure 82: Managing events (part 3)

- Please save the current scene as **chapter2_lose** (**File | Save Scene As**).

The last thing we have to do is to add this scene to the **Build Settings**:

- Please open the **Build Settings** (**File | Build Settings**).

- You will see that all the scenes from the first chapter are included; for now, you can unselect them (or remove them).

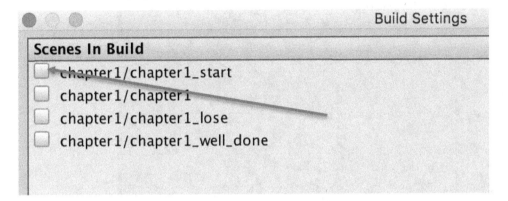

- You can then add the two scenes for this game (i.e., drag and drop them from the **Project** window), that is: **chapter2** and **chpater2_lose**, to the **Build Settings**.

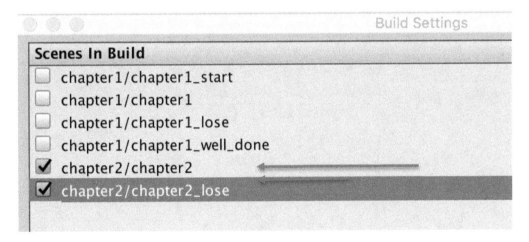

You can now save your scene, and open the scene **chapter2**, so that we can test what happens when the player enters an incorrect sequence.

- Please close the **Build Settings** window.

- Save your scene (**CTRL + S**).

- Open the scene **chapter2**.

- Play the scene.

As you play the scene, and enter an incorrect sequence, a new scene should appear with your score, and a button to restart the game, as illustrated in the next figure.

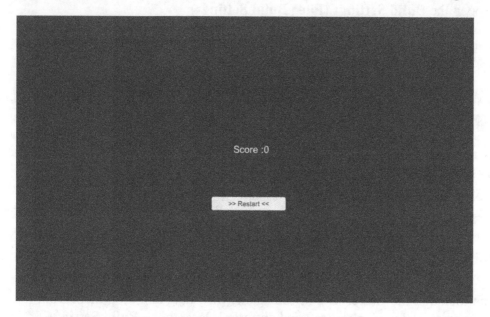

Figure 83: Restarting the game after an incorrect move

GENERATING SOUND EFFECTS

Ok, so the game works well at present; however, so that the users can obtain additional information on their move, we could add a few more features to our game, including:

- A Text field that displays the current score (or the number of colors that the player has managed to memorize so far).

- A specific sound for each of the colors, so that the player associates (and remembers) the colors associated to this sound.

So, first, let's create the onscreen text:

- Please open the scene called **chapter2**.

- Create a new **Text UI** object (i.e., select **GameObject | UI | Text**).

- Rename this object **nbMemorized**.

- Using the **Move** tool, you can move this object just above the boxes, as illustrated in the next figure.

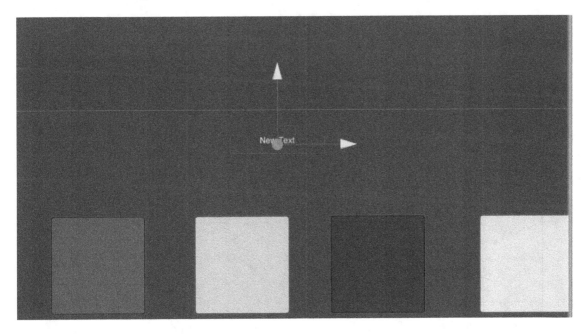

Figure 84: Moving the new text field

- Using the **Inspector**, in the component **Text**, please empty the attribute called **text**.

Figure 85: Emptying the text of the field

- You can also change its **color** to **white**, its **font size** to **20**, and its **alignment**, as illustrated on the next figure.

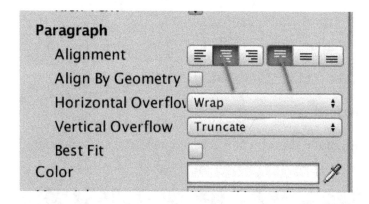

Figure 86: Changing the properties of the text.

Once this is done, we will create a function that displays the corresponding information in this text field.

- Please, open the script **ManageAudioGame**.

- Add the following function to this script.

```
public void updateUI()
{
    GameObject.Find ("nbMemorized").GetComponent<Text> ().text =
"" + indexOfColor;
}
```

- Please add the following code at the end of the **Start** function.

```
updateUI();
```

- Add the following code in the function **assessUserMove** (new code in bold).

```
if (allPerfect)
{
print ("WELL DONE!");
updateUI ();
return true;
}
else {print ("NOT RIGHT!"); return false;}
```

- In the previous code, we update the user interface when the user has guessed the sequence correctly.

- You can now save your script, play the scene, and check that your score is displayed at the top of the screen.

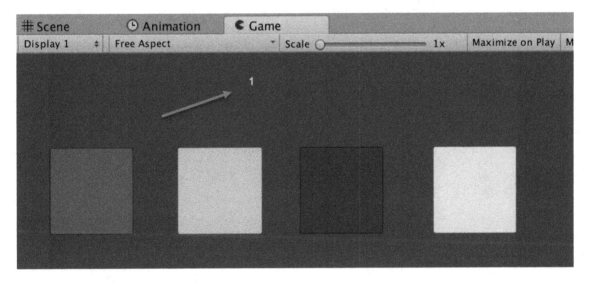

Figure 87: Checking the score

Once this is done, we can start to add some audio. For this, we will create a note for which the pitch will be linked to the label of the color being displayed, or the color chosen by the player. For this purpose, we will first create an **Audio Source** component, and then use it to generate a sound effect at run-time. So, let's get started!

- Please select the object **gameManager** in the **Hierarchy**.

- Add an **Audio Source** to it (i.e., select: **Component | Audio Source**).

- This should add an **Audio Source** component to the **gameManager** object.

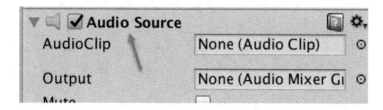

Figure 88: Adding an Audio Source

- Please import the sound called **bip** from the resource pack (i.e., drag and drop it from your file system to the **Project** window), and drag and drop it to the field called **AudioClip**.

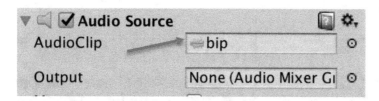

Figure 89: Adding a clip

- Also make sure that the option **Play on Awake** is set to **false**.

Figure 90: Amending the audio's properties

Once this is done, we can start to modify our script to be able to generate notes.

- Please open the script **ManageAudioGame**.

- Add the following function to it.

```
public void playNote(int index)
{
    float note = (float)index;
    GetComponent<AudioSource>().pitch = note;
    GetComponent<AudioSource>().Play();
}
```

In the previous code:

- We define a new note based on the tag of the corresponding box.

- The pitch of the sound is based on this note.

- We then play the sound at the pitch defined earlier.

Now that we have defined the function **playNote**, we can then call it whenever a box is displayed or when a box has been selected by the player.

- Please. add the following code at the beginning of the function **submitColor**.

```
playNote (newColor);
```

- Please add this code at the end of the function **displayBox**.

```
playNote(index);
```

- You can now save your script and test the scene; you will notice that a different sound is played every time a color is displayed or selected by the player.

If you would like to increase the quality of the audio played, you can also modify the function **playNote** as follows (new code in bold):

```
public void playNote(int index)
{
    float pitch = 0.5f;
    float note = (float)index;
    GetComponent<AudioSource> ().pitch = pitch * Mathf.Pow(2.0f,
(note)/12.0f);
    GetComponent<AudioSource>().Play();
}
```

In the previous code:

- We define a new pitch for the note to be played; the lower this number and the deeper the note.

- We also use some mathematics to calculate a new frequency based on the note and the tone.

You can now test your game, and hear the difference in the sound effects generated.

The last thing we need to do now is to be able to check whether the player is selecting the right color: at present we have to wait for the full sequence to be entered before completing the test. So, what we could do instead is to perform this check every time the player selects a box (instead of waiting for the player to enter a full sequence).

For this purpose, we will create a new function called **assessUserCurrentMove** and call it whenever the user has selected a box.

- Please open the script **ManageAudioGame**.

- Add the following function before the end of the class (i.e., before the last closing curly bracket).

```
public bool assessUserCurrentMove()
{
    if   (sequenceOfColorsSubmitted   [nbColorsSubmitted-1]   ==
sequenceOfColor [nbColorsSubmitted-1])
        return (true);
    else
    return false;

}
```

In the previous code:

- We define the function **assessUserCurrentMove**.

- We check if the color chosen by the player matches the corresponding color in the sequence created by the game.

Next, we will just need to modify the function **submitColor** as follows (new code in bold):

```
if (currentState == STATE_WAIT_FOR_USER_INPUT)
{

    sequenceOfColorsSubmitted [nbColorsSubmitted] = newColor;
    nbColorsSubmitted++;
    bool rightMove = assessUserCurrentMove ();
    if (!rightMove) loadLoseLevel();


    if (nbColorsSubmitted == (indexOfColor))
    {
        currentState = STATE_PROCESS_USER_INPUT;
    }

}
```

In the previous code, as we have done earlier, we check if the player's move is correct (i.e., right color selected) and then call the function **loadLoseLevel** otherwise.

You can test your scene and check that after an incorrect move, the game will display the scene called **lose**, without waiting for you to enter the complete sequence.

That's it!

LEVEL ROUNDUP

Well, this is it!

In this chapter, we have learned about creating a relatively simple memory game with interesting features such as: displaying or hiding objects, playing sounds and generating frequencies for this sound, creating a finite-state machine, arrays to store a sequence, and a timer to play this sequence. So, we have covered some significant ground compared to the last chapter.

Checklist

You can consider moving to the next chapter if you can do the following:

- Create a timer.

- Use switch statements to create different states for your game.

- Display or hide objects from your script.

Quiz

It's now time to check your knowledge with a quiz. So please try to answer the following questions (or specify whether the statements are correct or incorrect). The solutions are included in your resource pack. Good luck!

1. When using switch case statements, it is a good practice to add a **break** statements for each case.

2. The following code will create a constant variable.

```
private const int STATE_PLAY_SEQUENCE = 1;
```

3. The following code will hide an object.

```
GameObject.FindWithTag ("myObject").GetComponent<Image>().enabled
= false;
```

4. The following code will play a note, even if the object linked to this script does not have any **Audio Source** component.

```
GetComponent<AudioSource>().pitch = 2;
GetComponent<AudioSource>().Play();.
```

5. The following code will add one to the variable time every seconds.

```
float time + = Time.time;
```

6. The following code will create a new array of integers.

```
Int [] sequenceOfColor = new int[] { 1; 2; 3; 4 ;2};
```

7. The following function will be accessible from anywhere in the game

```
void test(){}
```

8. The following variable will be accessible from the **Inspector**.

```
int myVariable
```

9. Using the **Inspector**, it is possible to apply changes simultaneously to all objects selected, provided that they share the same attribute that you want to modify.

10. If you are using buttons in your game, the following code, if linked to a button, will return its name, when the button is pressed.

```
EventSystem.current.currentSelectedGameObject.name
```

Challenge 1

Now that you have managed to complete this chapter and that you have improved your skills, let's do the following.

- Modify the texture of each box so that, instead of displaying colored boxes, the game displays an image; this image would be different for each box.

- Add a splash-screen where the player can press on a start button to start the game; you can duplicate the scene **chapter2_lose** for this purpose.

ontper:

3
CREATING A CARD GUESSING GAME

In this section, we will create a simple card guessing game where the player has to remember a set of 20 cards and to match these cards based on their value.

After completing this chapter, you will be able to:

- Create a card game.
- Change the sprite of an object at run-time.
- Check when two cards picked by the player have the same value.
- Shuffle the cards.

INTRODUCTION

In this chapter, we will create a new card game as follows:

- The deck of cards will be shuffled.

- There will be two rows of cards (i.e., 10 cards in each row).

- All cards are initially hidden.

- The player needs to pick one card from the first row and then one card from the second row.

- If the cards are identical, it's a match, and they are then both removed.

- Otherwise both cards are hidden again.

- The player wins when s/he has managed to match (and subsequently remove) all the cards.

Figure 91: An example of the game completed

SETTING-UP THE INTERFACE

First, we will import the new deck of cards:

- Please save your current scene (**File | Save Scene**).

- Create a new scene (**File | New Scene**).

- Save this new scene as **chapter3**.

- As we have done before, you can remove the skybox used for the background (if any), using the menu **Window | Lighting**.

- Please locate the resource pack that you have downloaded in your file system, and import (i.e., drag and drop) the folder called **cards** to the **Project** window in Unity.

- As you will see, this folder includes a set of 68 cards that we will be using for our game, as illustrated in the next figure.

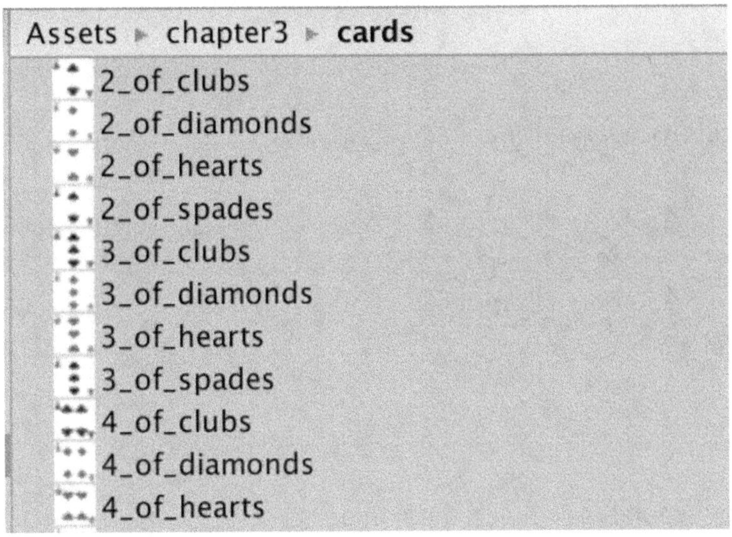

Figure 92: Importing the cards

- Once this is done, we just need to change some of the properties of these images so that they can be used as sprites in our game.

- In the **Project** window, and in the folder called **cards**, that contains the different images imported, please select all the cards (i.e., click on one card and then select **CTRL + A**).

- Using the **Inspector**, change the **Texture Type** of these images to **Sprite (2D and UI)** and leave the other options as default, as described on the next figure.

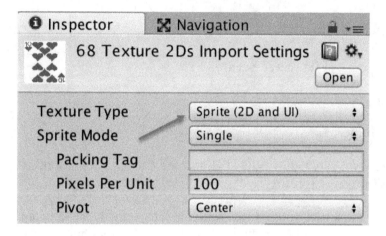

Figure 93: Changing the attribute Texture Type

- You can then press the **Apply** button located in the bottom-right corner of the window, as described on the next figure.

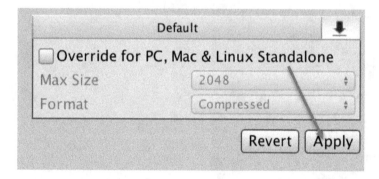

Figure 94: Applying changes

- It should take Unity a few seconds to convert these images.

Next, we will use one of these sprites to start to implement basic functionalities for our game.

- Please create a new square sprite: from the **Project** window select **Create | Sprites | Square**.

- Rename this new asset **tile** and drag and drop it to the **Scene** view, as illustrated on the next figure.

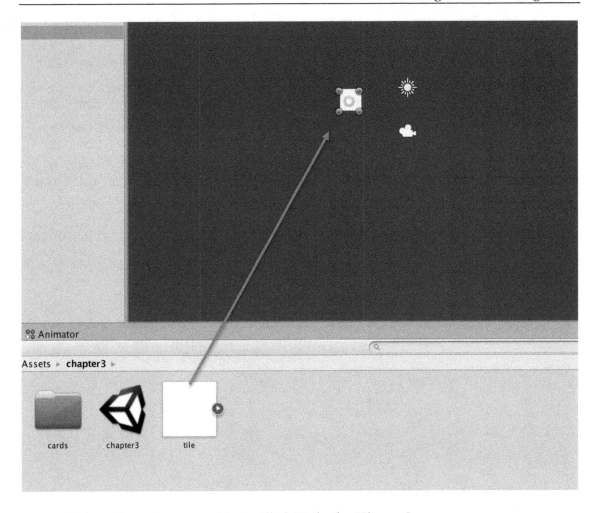

- This will create a new object called **tile** in the **Hierarchy**.

- You can change its position to **(0, 0, 0)** and add a **2D Box Collider** component to it: from the top menu select **Component | Physics2D | Box 2D Collider**.

- This collider is needed so that we can detect clicks on this sprite.

Next, we will create a script that will process clicks on this sprite.

- Please create a new C# script called **Tile** (i.e., from the **Project** window, select **Create | C# Script**).

- Open this script.

- Add the following function to it.

```
public void OnMouseDown()
{

    print ("You pressed on tile");

}
```

- Save your script, and drag and drop it to the object called **tile** in the **Hierarchy**.

Once this is done, you can test the scene by playing the scene and by then clicking on the white rectangle (tile) that you have created; a message should appear in the **Console** window.

Next, we will just change the appearance of our tile by using one of the sprites that we have imported.

- Please select the object called **tile** in the **Hierarchy**.

- Using the **Inspector**, you will see that it has a component called **Sprite Renderer**, with an attribute called **Sprite**, as described on the next figure.

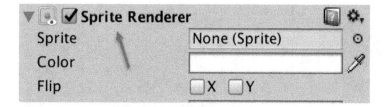

Figure 95: Identifying the Sprite Renderer component

- Drag and drop one of the images that you have imported from the **Project** window (i.e., from the folder called **cards**) to the attribute called **Sprite**, for example the **two of hearts**, as illustrated in the next figure.

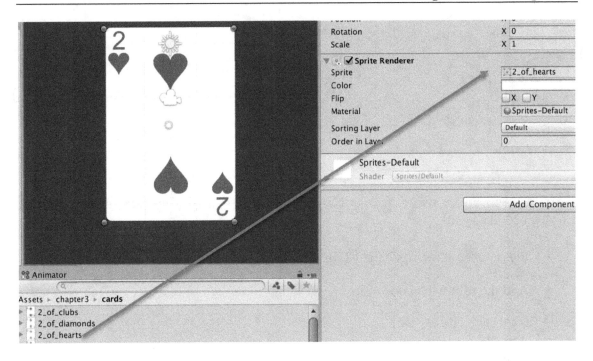

- Once this is done, you should see that the tile has now turned into a card, as per the previous figure.

Next, we will create the code that either hides or displays a card; for this purpose, we will be using two different sprites: the sprite for the card that is supposed to be displayed, and a blank sprite that symbolizes the back of each card, for when a card is supposed to be hidden.

- Please add the following code at the beginning of the class **Tile**.

```
private bool tileRevealed = false;
public Sprite originalSprite;
public Sprite hiddenSprite;
```

- Because the last two variables (i.e., **originalSprite** and **hiddenSprite**) are public, if you select the object called **tile** in the **Hierarchy** and look at the **Inspector**, you should now see that its component called **Tile** has two empty fields (or placeholders) called **originalSprite** and **hiddenSprite**.

- Please drag and drop the sprite called **2_of_hearts** from the **Project** window to the field **originalSprite**, and the sprite called **back_of_cards** to the field called **hiddenSprite**.

- The component should then look as in the next figure.

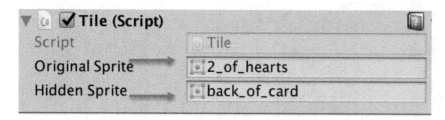

Figure 96: Setting the appearance of the card.

Next, we will create two functions called **hideCard** and **displayCard** that will either display or hide a card.

- Please open the script called **Tile**.

- Add the following code to it.

```
public void hideCard()
{
    GetComponent<SpriteRenderer> ().sprite = hiddenSprite;
    tileRevealed = false;
}
public void revealCard()
{
    GetComponent<SpriteRenderer> ().sprite = originalSprite;
    tileRevealed = true;
}
```

In the previous code, we create two functions that either display or hide a card by setting the sprite for this particular card to the **hiddenSprite** or the **originalSprite**. The variable **tileRevealed** is also amended to indicate whether the card is displayed or hidden.

- Next, add the following code to the **Start** function, so that all cards are initially hidden at the start of the game.

```
hideCard();
```

- Last, we can modify the function **OnMouseDown** as follows:

```
public void OnMouseDown()
{
    print ("You pressed on tile");
    if (tileRevealed)
        hideCard ();
    else
        revealCard ();
}
```

In the previous code:

- When the mouse is clicked, we check whether the card is currently revealed or hidden.

- If it is revealed, then we call the function **hideCard**.

- Otherwise, we call the function **revealCard**.

You can now save your code, and test the scene; you should see that the card is hidden at the beginning (i.e., the back of the card is displayed); then, as you click several times on the card, it should subsequently be hidden or revealed.

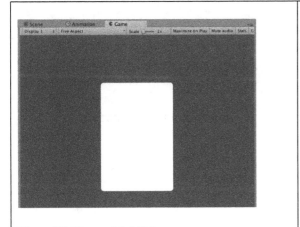

Figure 97: The card is hidden

Figure 98: The card is displayed

- Lastly, we will scale down the card: using the **Inspector**, modify the scale property of the object **tile** to (0.5, 0.5, 1).

Now that the interaction with the card works, we can create a prefab from it, so that this prefab can be used to generate several similar cards.

- Please select the object **tile** in the **Hierarchy**.

- Drag and drop it to the **Project** window.

- This should create a new **prefab** called **tile**, as illustrated on the next figure.

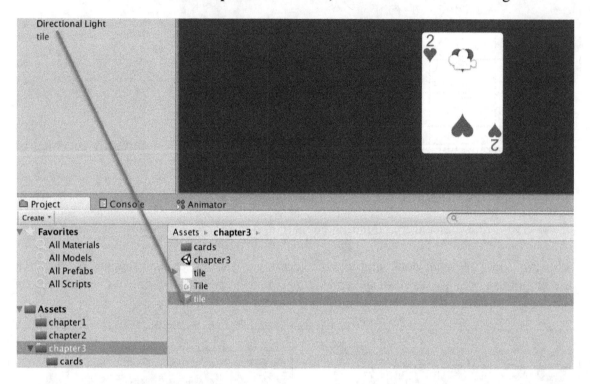

Figure 99: Creating a prefab from the card

- You can then delete or de-activate the object called **tile** in the **Hierarchy**.

CREATING A GAME MANAGER

So at this stage, we have managed to create a card (and a corresponding prefab) that we can either hide or reveal. So the next step will be to display several cards and make it possible for the player to match them. For this purpose, we will create an empty object **gameManager** that will manage the game, including adding cards to the game.

- Please create a new empty object (**GameObject | Create Empty**), and rename it **gameManager**.

- Using the **Project** view, create a new script called **ManageCards** (i.e., from the **Project** window, select **Create | C# Script**), and drag and drop it on the object called **gameManager**.

- Open the script called **ManageCards** (i.e., double-click on it in the **Project** window).

- Add this code at the beginning of the script (new code in bold).

```
public GameObject card;
void Start ()
{
    displayCards();
}
public void displayCards()
{
    Instantiate    (card,    new    Vector3    (0,    0,    0),
Quaternion.identity);
}
```

In the previous code:

- We declare a new variable called **card**, that is public (hence accessible from the **Inspector** window), and that will be used as a template for all the cards to be added to the game (i.e., it will be based on the template called **tile**).

- We also create a function called **displayCards**.

- This function instantiates a new card.

Before we can test this code, we just need to initialize the variable **card**, as follows:

- Please select the object **gameManager** in the **Hierarchy**.

- Drag and drop the prefab called **tile** to the field called **card**, in the component called **ManageCards**, as illustrated on the next figure.

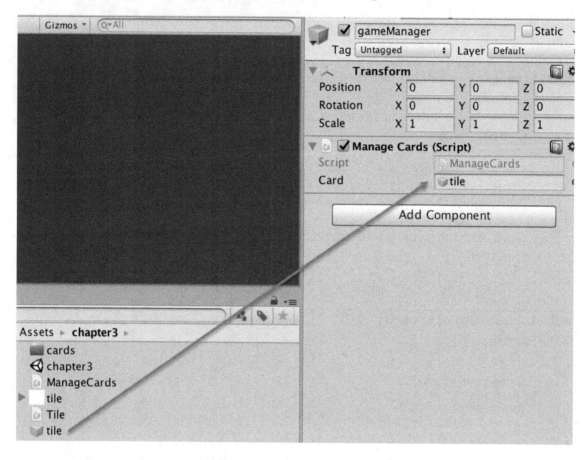

Figure 100: Initializing the variable called card

- Once this is done, you can test the game by playing the scene; you should see that a card has been added to the game, as described in the next figure.

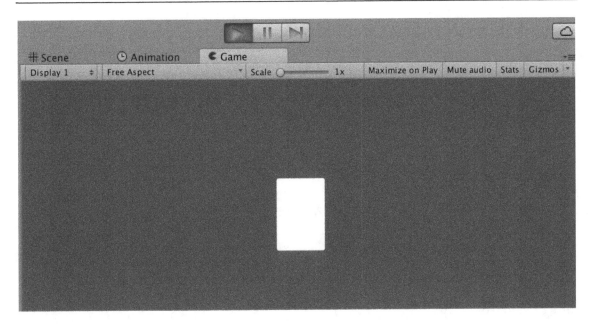

Figure 101: Testing the game

If you find it difficult to select (i.e., click on) some of the cards, it may be because their collider is too small and needs to be resized, hence collision and clicks might only be detected on a portion of the card rather than on the entire card.

Next, we will modify the script called **Tile**, to add a function that will set the sprite (or image) that should be displayed when this card is revealed; this is because in the next section, the cards will be allocated randomly; so we will no longer set the sprite for each card manually; instead, this will be done through our code.

- Please open the script called **Tile**.

- Add the following function to it.

```
public void setOriginalSprite(Sprite newSprite)
{
    originalSprite = newSprite;
}
```

In the previous code, we create a public function that will be accessible from outside this class and that will change the original sprite for this card to a sprite that is passed as a parameter to the function.

- Please save this script (i.e., the script called **Tile**).

- Please open the script **ManageCards**.

- Add the following function to the class.

```
void addACard(int rank)
{
    GameObject c = (GameObject)(Instantiate (card, new Vector3
(0, 0, 0), Quaternion.identity));
}
```

In the previous code:

- We declare a function called **addACard.**

- This function creates a new card.

- We can now modify the function called **displayCards** as follows:

```
public void displayCards()
{
    //Instantiate    (card,    new    Vector3    (0,    0,    0),
Quaternion.identity);
    addACard(0);
}
```

ADDING MULTIPLE CARDS AUTOMATICALLY

We will now create several cards on the go. The idea will be to display two rows of 10 cards each. The player will then need to match cards from the first row to cards on the second row. So the idea will be to:

- Create and add new cards based on the prefab created earlier.

- Arrange the cards so that they are aligned around the center of the screen and all visible onscreen.

- For each card, set the default sprite that should be displayed when the card is revealed.

- Shuffle the cards.

So the first step will be to add all of these cards.

If you look at the sprites that we have imported in the **Project** window, you will notice that their size is 500 by 725 pixels; we have also scaled-down these images using the **Inspector**, so their actual width in the game is 250 pixels; if you remember well, we used an import setting of 100 pixel per units pixels; this means that our cards will have a size of 2.5 (i.e., 250/100) in the game's units. So when creating our cards, we will need to make sure that their origins (or center) is at least 2.5 units apart (we will choose 3 units to be safe).

- In the script called **ManageCards**, please modify the function **AddAcard** as follows (new code in bold):

```
void addACard(int rank)
{
    //GameObject c = (GameObject)(Instantiate (card, new Vector3
(0, 0, 0), Quaternion.identity));
    GameObject c = (GameObject)(Instantiate (card, new Vector3
(rank*3.0f, 0, 0), Quaternion.identity));
}
```

In the previous code, we make sure that the x coordinate of the new card will be based on its rank; as we will be adding other cards, the first card's x coordinate will be 3 (i.e., 1 x 3), the second card's x coordinate will be 6 (i.e., 2 x 3), and so on.

- Next, we can modify the function called **displayCards** so that we can add a row of 10 cards, with the following code (new code in bold).

```
public void displayCards()
{
    //Instantiate    (card,    new    Vector3    (0,    0,    0),
Quaternion.identity);
    //addACard(0);
    for (int i = 0; i < 10; i++)
    {
        addACard (i);
    }
}
```

- Please save your code and play the scene; you will notice that 10 cards have been created; however, some of them are outside the screen; in other words, the cards need to be centered around the center of the screen.

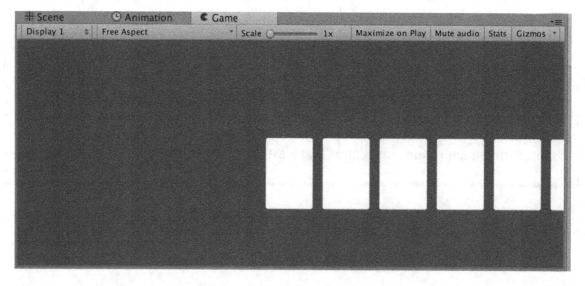

Figure 102: Displaying 10 cards

So, to solve this issue, we will do the following:

- Create an empty object that will be used as an anchor for the cards.

- Move this object to the center of the screen.

- Center the cards horizontally around this object.

So let's proceed.

- Please create an empty object and call it **centerOfScreen**.

- Using the **Inspector**, change its position to **(0, 0, 0)**.

- Open the script **ManageCards** and modify the function **addACard** as follows (new code in bold):

```
void addACard(int rank)
{

    GameObject cen = GameObject.Find("centerOfScreen");
    Vector3 newPosition = new Vector3 (cen.transform.position.x
+       ((rank-10/2)       *3),        cen.transform.position.y,
cen.transform.position.z);
    GameObject c = (GameObject)(Instantiate (card, newPosition,
Quaternion.identity));

    //GameObject c = (GameObject)(Instantiate (card, new Vector3
(0, 0, 0), Quaternion.identity));
    //GameObject c = (GameObject)(Instantiate (card, new Vector3
(rank*3.0f, 0, 0), Quaternion.identity));
}
```

As you save the code and play the scene, you should see that the cards are now centered; however, their size is too large for all of them to fit onscreen; so we will need to resize the cards accordingly.

Figure 103: Displaying 10 aligned cards

- Using the **Inspector**, change the scale of the **tile** prefab to **(0.3, 0.3, 0.3)**.

- Open the script called **ManageCards** and modify it as follows (new code in bold):

```
void addACard(int rank)
{


    float cardOriginalScale = card.transform.localScale.x;
    float scaleFactor = (500 * cardOriginalScale) / 100.0f;


    GameObject cen = GameObject.Find("centerOfScreen");
    //Vector3         newPosition         =         new         Vector3
(cen.transform.position.x         +         ((rank-10/2)         *3),
cen.transform.position.y, cen.transform.position.z);
    Vector3 newPosition = new Vector3 (cen.transform.position.x
+     ((rank-10/2)     *scaleFactor),     cen.transform.position.y,
cen.transform.position.z);


    GameObject c = (GameObject)(Instantiate (card, newPosition,
Quaternion.identity));
```

In the previous code:

- We save the initial scale of the card.

- We create a variable called **scaleFactor** that takes into account the original width of the card (i.e., **500**) as well as its original scale.

- This **scaleFactor** variable is taken into account when defining the x coordinate of each card.

Please save your code, and play the scene; you should see that now all cards are displayed within the camera's field of view, as illustrated in the next figure.

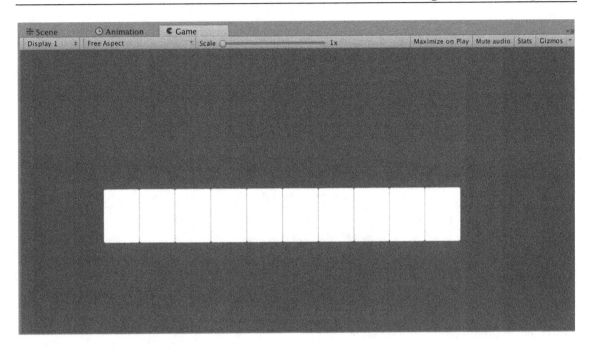

Figure 104: Displaying and scaling the cards

ASSOCIATING THE CORRECT IMAGE TO EACH CARD

At this stage, we can display the hidden cards, however, their value is the same (i.e., they are all showing the same sprite); if you play the scene and click on each of the images, they will all display the **2 of hearts**, as illustrated on the next figure.

Figure 105: Displaying cards with a similar image

So, the idea now is to specify a corresponding sprite for each card; so we will do the following:

- Create 10 tags.

- Assign a tag to each of these cards based on their rank (e.g., first card from the left will use the tag called **1**, the second card from the left will use the tag called **2**, and so on).

- Associate an image to each card based on its tag (e.g., **ace for tag 1**, **two for tag 2**, and so on).

So let's proceed:

- Please select the prefab called **tile** in the **Project** window.

- Using the **Inspector**, click to the right of the label called **Tag**.

Figure 106: Checking tags already created

If you find it difficult to select (i.e., click on) some of the cards, it may be because their collider is too small and needs to be resized, hence collision and clicks might only be detected on a portion of the card rather than on the entire card.

- If you have already completed the previous chapters, you should see that the tags **1**, **2**, **3**, and **4** have already been created; if not, we can create these in the next steps.

- Please click on **Add Tag**.

Figure 107: Creating tags

- In the next window, please click several times on the button +, as illustrated in the next figure.

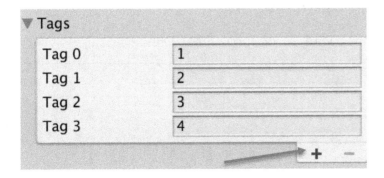

- This will create new fields that you can use to create additional tags, by typing a number (for a new tag) to the right of the fields which name starts with **Tag,** as illustrated on the next figure.

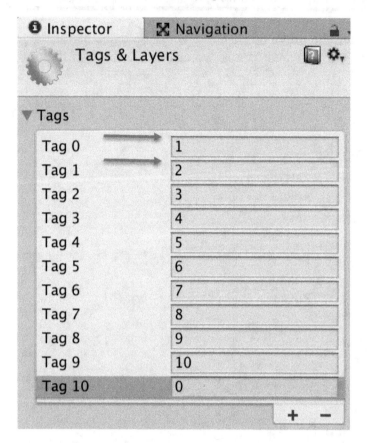

Figure 108: Creating the 11 tags

- Once this is done, you should have **11** tags ranging from **0** to **10**, as per the previous figure.

We can then use these tags from our code.

- Please open the script called **ManageCards**.

- Add the following code at the end of the function **addACard**.

```
c.tag = ""+rank;
```

- Please save your code.

As you play the scene, and if you click on one of the cards that has been created in the **Hierarchy**, you will see, using the **Inspector** that each card has a tag that ranges from **0** to **9**.

Note that tags cannot be created from a script; they have to have already been defined in the editor before they can be applied to objects in a script.

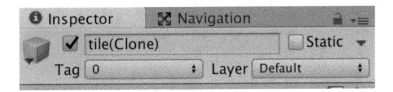

Figure 109:Checking the new tags

Next, we will work on the images that need to be displayed when a card is revealed. For this, we will access the images that we have imported in our project directly from our script; so the next steps will consist in:

- Moving all the images that we have imported to a "recognized" or "standard" folder that we can access from our script.

- Accessing the images from this folder.

- Associating a corresponding image based on the rank of the card created.

So let's proceed:

If you have already completed the previous chapters, then you would already have created a **Resources** folder (within the **Assets** folder), as illustrated in the next figure.

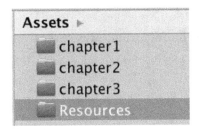

Figure 110: Checking the folder Resources

If this is not the case, we can create this folder as follows:

- In the **Project** window, select the folder called **Assets**.

- Then, from the **Project** window, select **Create | Folder**.

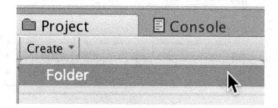

Figure 111: Creating a new folder

- Rename the new folder **Resources** (i.e., right-click on the folder and then select the option **Rename**).

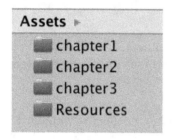

Figure 112: Renaming the folder

Now that this folder has been created, you can move the images that you have imported inside this folder, within Unity, as follows:

- Within Unity, navigate to the folder called **cards** where all the cards have been stored previously.

- Select all the cards (i.e., **CTRL + A**).

- Move these cards (i.e., drag and drop them) to the folder called **Resources**, as illustrated in the next figure.

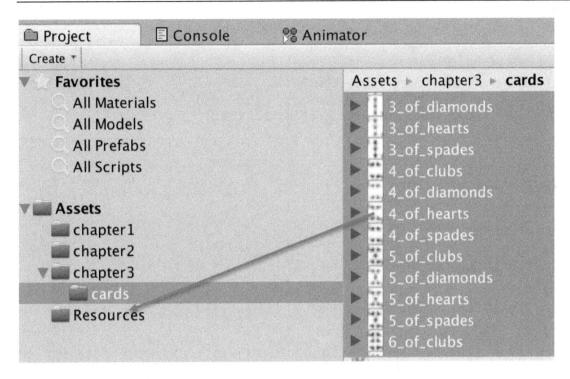

Figure 113: Moving the images to the Resources folder

- If you then check the content of the folder called **Resources**, you should see that the cards were moved successfully, as illustrated in the next figure.

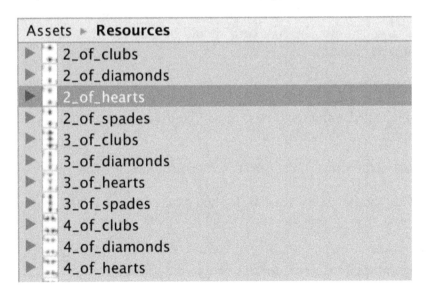

Figure 114: Checking that the cards have been copied properly

Next, we will modify the script **ManageCards** so that the correct images from the **Resources** folder are assigned to each card.

- Please open the script **ManageCards**.

- Add this code at the end of the function **addACard**.

```
c.name = "" + rank;
string nameOfCard = "";
string cardNumber = "";
if (rank == 0)
     cardNumber = "ace";
else
     cardNumber = "" + (rank+1);
nameOfCard = cardNumber + "_of_hearts";
Sprite s1 = (Sprite) (Resources.Load<Sprite>(nameOfCard));
print ("S1:" + s1);
GameObject.Find(""+rank).GetComponent<Tile>  ().setOriginalSprite
(s1);
```

In the previous code:

- The name of the sprite to be selected for a particular card will be in the form: **XX_of_hearts**; where **XX** can be a number (e.g., 1, 2, 3, 4, 5, 6, etc.) or a string (e.g., ace). So the purpose of this code is to form this word based on the card that we have just added and its rank; the first card should be the **ace of hearts**, the second card a **2 of heart**s, and so on.

- We set the name of the new card.

- We declare a variable called **nameOfCard** that will be used to save the name of the corresponding sprite for a particular card.

- We form the first part of the name of the card based on its rank.

- Once the name of the sprite to be used is formed properly and stored in the variable **nameOfCard**, we access the corresponding sprite and save it in the variable called **s1**.

- We then set the **originalSprite** variable for this card to the sprite **s1**.

You can now save your code, and test the scene. You should see that if you click on each of the cards, they will show the correct image.

Figure 115: Displaying all the cards.

SHUFFLING THE CARDS

Now we just need to be able to shuffle the cards; the idea will be to create two rows of cards with identical sets of cards but shuffled. So we will create a new function that will shuffle the cards for us, and then call it from the **Start** function, after the cards have been added to the game view.

To do so, we need to differentiate between the order in which the cards are picked (this will determine their position) and their value (this will determine the value of the card and the corresponding sprite).

- Please create the following function in the class **ManageCards**.

```
public int [] createShuffledArray()
{
    int [] newArray = new int [] {0,1,2,3,4,5,6,7,8,9};
    int tmp;
    for (int t = 0; t < 10; t++ )
    {
        tmp = newArray[t];
        int r = Random.Range(t, 10);
        newArray[t] = newArray[r];
        newArray[r] = tmp;
    }
    return newArray;
}
```

In the previous code:

- We declare a new function called **createShuffledArray**; it returns an array of integers for which the values are shuffled.

- We declare a new array of integers that includes the labels of all 10 cards; these values are ordered in ascending order.

- We then loop through this array and shuffle its content.

- Once this is done, we return an array that includes these values in a random order.

This shuffling function is based on the Fisher-Yates algorithm.

Next, we will need to modify the function **addACard** so that it accounts for a card's rank and its value:

- Please modify the definition of the function **addACard** as follows:

```
void addACard(int rank, int value)
```

- Modify the function **addACard** as follows (new code in bold):

```
c.tag = ""+(value+1);
c.name = "" + value;
string nameOfCard = "";
string cardNumber = "";
if (value == 0)
    cardNumber = "ace";
else
    cardNumber = "" + (value+1);
nameOfCard = cardNumber + "_of_hearts";
Sprite s1 = (Sprite) (Resources.Load<Sprite>(nameOfCard));
GameObject.Find(""+value).GetComponent<Tile> ().setOriginalSprite
(s1);
```

- Last, we will modify the function **displayCards** as follows (new code in bold):

```
int [] shuffledArray = createShuffledArray();
for (int i = 0; i < 10; i++)
{
    //addACard (i);
    addACard (i,shuffledArray[i]);
}
```

- Please save your script and test the game; you should see that, after clicking on some of the cards, that these cards have been shuffled, as described on the next figure.

Figure 116: Displaying the card (after shuffling)

If you find it difficult to select (i.e., click on) some of the cards, it may be because their collider is too small and needs to be resized, hence collision and clicks might only be detected on a portion of the card rather than on the entire card.

Last but not least, we want to create two rows of cards. So it will be the same as we have done so far, except that we will modify the function **addACard** so that we can specify the row where the card should be added (i.e., first or second row).

- Please change the definition of the function **addACard** as follows (new code in bold):

```
void addACard(int row, int rank, int value)
{
```

In the previous code, we have modified the function so that it takes a third parameter named **row**.

- Next, please modify the function **displayCards** as follows (new code in bold):

```
int [] shuffledArray = createShuffledArray();
int [] shuffledArray2 = createShuffledArray();
for (int i = 0; i < 10; i++)
{
//addACard (i);
    addACard (0, i, shuffledArray[i]);
    addACard (1, i, shuffledArray2[i]);


}
```

In the previous code:

- We declare another array of integers called **shuffledArray2**, that will be used for the second row of cards.

- In the **for** loop, we then call the function **addACard** to display both the first and the second row.

- When the function **addACard** is called, three parameters are passed: the **row** (0 or 1), the **rank** of the card (i.e., its **position** in the row), and its value (i.e., ace, 1, or 2, etc.).

Next, we can modify the function **addACard** as follows:

```
//Vector3 newPosition = new Vector3 (cen.transform.position.x +
((rank-10/2)        *scaleFactor),        cen.transform.position.y,
cen.transform.position.z);
float yScaleFactor = (725 * cardOriginalScale) / 100.0f;
Vector3 newPosition = new Vector3 (cen.transform.position.x +
((rank-10/2) *scaleFactor), cen.transform.position.y + ((row-2/2)
*yScaleFactor), cen.transform.position.z);
```

In the previous code:

- We comment the previous line that was used to set the new position of the card.

- We define a new variable called **yScaleFactor** that will be used to calculate the position of the card (especially its y coordinate).

- We then define the new position of the card using the parameter called **row** and the variable called **yScaleFactor** to centre it properly.

Next, we just need to change the naming of the new card.

- Please replace this code:

```
c.name = "" + value;
```

- ...with this code...

```
c.name = ""+row+"_"+value;
```

In the previous code, we specify that the cards from the first row have a name starting with 0 (**row = 0**) and that the cards from the second row have a name starting with 1 (i.e., **row = 1**).

- Please replace this code...

```
GameObject.Find(""+value).GetComponent<Tile> ().setOriginalSprite
(s1);
```

- ... with this code

```
GameObject.Find(""+row+"_"+value).GetComponent<Tile>
().setOriginalSprite (s1);
```

- Please save your code.

As you play the scene, you should now have two rows of cards, as illustrated on the next figure.

Figure 117: Displaying two rows of cards

If you find it difficult to select (i.e., click on) some of the cards, it may be because their collider is too small and needs to be resized, hence collision and clicks might only be detected on a portion of the card rather than on the entire card.

So, in this case you can resize the collider as follows:

- Select the prefab called **tile** in the **Project** window.

- Scroll down to the component called **Box Collider 2D**.

- Change the size of the collider to (**x=5, y = 7**).

ALLOWING THE PLAYER TO CHOOSE CARDS FROM EACH ROW

So now that we can shuffle and display two rows of 10 cards, we just need to make it possible for the player to select a card from the first row, then a card from the second row, and then check if these cards are similar (i.e., have the same value) by comparing their tags and value.

Based on our code, we know that the cards from the first row have a name starting with **0** and that cards from the second row have a name starting with **1**, as illustrated in the next figure.

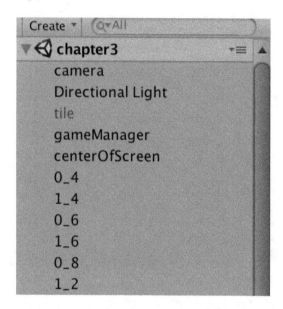

Figure 118: Naming the cards

If you find it difficult to select (i.e., click on) some of the cards, it may be because their collider is too small and needs to be resized, hence collision and clicks might only be detected on a portion of the card rather than on the entire card.

So we will proceed as follows:

- Display the cards (i.e., two rows).

- Allow the player to successively pick (i.e., click on) two cards.

- We will then check that whenever the player clicks on a card for the first time, that the name of this card includes **0** (i.e. that it belongs to the first row).

- We will also check that whenever the player clicks on a second card, that the name of this card includes **1** (i.e. that it belongs to the second row).

- After that we will compare their tags.

- If these cards have the same tag (i.e., the same value) then both will be destroyed.

Next, we can implement the code that checks how we handle clicks on cards.

- Please add the following code at the start of the script **ManageCards**.

```
private bool firstCardSelected, secondCardSelected;
private GameObject card1, card2;
```

- Please add the following code just before the end of the class.

```
public void cardSelected(GameObject card)
{
    if (!firstCardSelected)
    {
        firstCardSelected = true;
        card1 = card;
        card1.GetComponent<Tile> ().revealCard ();
    }
}
```

In the previous code:

- We declare a new function called **cardSelected**; this function will be used to monitor whether we have already selected the first card.

- If this is not the case, then the card that was passed as a parameter (i.e., the card currently selected – the first card -) is saved in the variable **card1**.

- We also display (i.e., reveal) the value of this card.

The hiding and revealing of the cards will now be handled by the game manager; so we will modify the function called **OnMouseDown** in the **Tile** class, as follows:

```
public void OnMouseDown()
{
    print ("You pressed on tile");
    /*if (tileRevealed)
        hideCard ();
    else
        revealCard ();*/
    GameObject.Find    ("gameManager").GetComponent<ManageCards>
().cardSelected (gameObject);
}
```

In the previous code:

- We comment the previous code.

- Now, when the player clicks on a card, the function called **cardSelected** (that we have defined earlier), is called.

- The card that the player has just selected is also passed as a parameter.

Next, we will further code the overall management of the game.

- Please add the following code at the beginning of the class called **ManageCards**.

```
private string rowForCard1, rowForCard2;
```

- Modify the function **cardSelected** as follows:

```
public void cardSelected(GameObject card)
{
    if (!firstCardSelected)
    {
        string row = card.name.Substring (0, 1);
        rowForCard1 = row;
        firstCardSelected = true;
        card1 = card;
        card1.GetComponent<Tile> ().revealCard ();
    }
    else if (firstCardSelected && !secondCardSelected)
    {
        string row = card.name.Substring (0, 1);
        rowForCard2 = row;
        if (rowForCard2 != rowForCard1)
        {
            card2 = card;
            secondCardSelected = true;
            card2.GetComponent<Tile> ().revealCard ();
        }
    }
}
```

In the previous code:

- If the player selects the first card, we record the name of the row for this card, we save this card in the variable **card1**, and we also reveal the card.

- Then, if the player is selecting the second card, we record the name of the row for this card, and check that it is a different row than the first card selected.

- If this is the case, then we save this card in the variable **card2**, and reveal this card also.

- We also check whether we have a match, using the function **checkCard** that we yet have to create.

You can save both scripts now (i.e., **Tile** and **ManageCards**), and test the scene; as you try to select two cards, you should only be able to choose one card from the first row and a second card from the second row (or vice versa).

Figure 119: Picking one card from each row

CHECKING FOR A MATCH

Now we just need to determine when there is a match between the two cards selected by the player. In this case, we will delete both cards.

First let's create a function called **checkCards**; this function will check whether the two cards selected by the player are identical; if this is the case, they will be destroyed; otherwise, they will be hidden again; the checking will happen after a slight pause, so that the player can see the cards that have been selected before they are hidden again (if this is the case).

- Please add the following function to the class **ManageCards**:

```
public void checkCards()
{
    runTimer ();
}
```

In this function we call another function called **runTimer** (that we yet have to create).

- Please add the following code at the beginning of the class.

```
bool timerHasElapsed, timerHasStarted;
float timer;
```

In the previous code:

- The new variables defined will be employed to create a timer that will be used to pause after the second card has been collected.

- **timerHasElapsed** will be used to know whether the **pause time** has elapsed.

- **timerHasStarted** is used to determine whether the timer has already been started.

- The variable **timer** will be used to count the number of seconds between when the second card has been selected and when we start to compare the two cards.

Please add the following function to the class:

```
public void runTimer()
{
    timerHasElapsed = false;
    timerHasStarted = true;
}
```

In the previous code, we just initialise the timer and the associated variables.

Next, we will create and implement the timer; it will be done in the **Update** function; the timer will increase until it reaches **2** seconds; after two seconds, we will start to compare the two cards.

- Please add the following code to the **Update** function.

```
void Update ()
{
    if (timerHasStarted)
    {
        timer += Time.deltaTime;
        print (timer);
        if (timer >= 1) {
            timerHasElapsed = true;
            timerHasStarted = false;
            if (card1.tag == card2.tag) {
                Destroy (card1);
                Destroy (card2);
            } else {
                card1.GetComponent<Tile> ().hideCard ();
                card2.GetComponent<Tile> ().hideCard ();
            }
            firstCardSelected = false;
            secondCardSelected = false;
            card1 = null;
            card2 = null;
            rowForCard1 = "";
            rowForCard2 = "";
            timer = 0;
        }
    }
}
```

In the previous code

- We check if the timer has started.

- We then check whether the timer has started and that we have reached the end of the pause.

- In this case, we reinitialize the timer (using the variables **timerHasElapsed** and **timerHasStarted**).

- We check if the cards match and destroy (or hide) them both if we have a match.

- We then initialise the variable linked to the card selection, so that the player can restart the process of selecting two cards.

- Last, please check that the function **cardSelected** includes a call to the function **checkCards**, as highlighted in the next code (in bold).

```
secondCardSelected = true;
card2 = card;
card2.GetComponent<Tile> ().revealCard ();
checkCards ();
```

- Please save the code and test the game.

You should see that as you select one card from each row: if they match, then they should destroyed after a few seconds.

Figure 120: The game after two cards were matched

Next we will add a sound when the player has managed to match two cards:

- Please add an **AudioSource** component to the object **gameManager** (i.e., select: **Component | Audio | AudioSource**).

- Import the audio file called **ok.mp3** from the resource pack to the Unity **Project** window.

- Drag and drop this audio clip from the **Project** window to the **AudioClip** attribute of the component **Audio Source** for the object **gameManager**, as illustrated in the next figure.

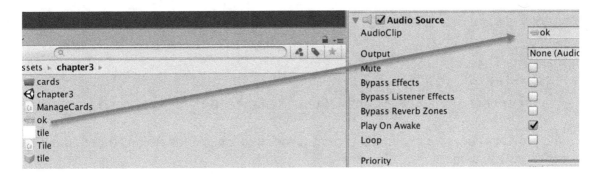

Figure 121: Adding an Audio Clip to the Audio Source

- Set the attribute **Play on Awake** to false.

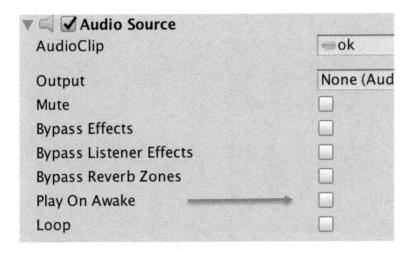

Figure 122: Setting the attribute Play on Awake

Next, we need to check how many cards the player has managed to match.

- Please, add this code at the beginning of the class **ManageCards**:

```
int nbMatch = 0;
```

- Add this code at the beginning of the script.

```
using UnityEngine.SceneManagement;
```

- Modify the function **Update** as follows (new code in bold).

```
Destroy (card1);
Destroy (card2);
nbMatch++;
if (nbMatch == 10)
    SceneManager.LoadScene (SceneManager.GetActiveScene().name);
```

In the previous code, we reload the current scene if the player has managed to find the 10 sets of identical cards.

LEVEL ROUNDUP

Summary

In this chapter, we have managed to create a challenging card game and we have learned some interesting skills too, including: hiding or revealing sprites, setting sprites or scaling images at run-time.

Checklist

You can consider moving to the next stage if you can do the following:

- Understand how to access sprites from a script.

- Understand how to create an array of integers.

- Know how to use the **substring** function.

Quiz

Now, let's check your knowledge! Please answer the following questions (the answers are included in the resource pack) or specify whether they are correct or incorrect.

1. To select all the assets in a given folder, you can just press CTRL + A.

2. To be able to detect clicks on a sprite, this sprite needs to have a collider.

3. The function **OnClick** is called automatically when the player clicks on an object if this function is added to a script linked to this object.

4. To create an empty object, you can select: **GameObject | Create | Empty Object**.

5. If a sprite with a width of 200 pixels is imported in Unity, and the **Import Settings** are **100 pixels per unit**, then this sprite will be 2 units-wide in the game.

6. In Unity, it is possible to use tags that have been created in other scenes in the same project.

7. The following code will save a sprite that is stored in the folder called **Resources**.

```
Sprite s1 = (Sprite) (Resources.Load<Sprite>("mySprite"));
```

8. The following code will create an array of 10 integers.

```
int [] newArray = new int [] {0,1,2,3,4,5,6,7,8,9};
```

9. If a function is declared as **public**, it cannot be accessible from outside the class.

10. For an **Audio Source** component, the attribute **Play on Awake** is set to true by default in Unity.

Challenge 1

For this chapter, your challenge will be to modify the game as follows:

- Change the color of the cards chosen for each row (i.e., hearts for first row and spades for the second row).
- Display the number of correct matches onscreen.

4
CREATING A PUZZLE GAME

In this section, we will be creating a game where the player has to complete a puzzle by moving the corresponding pieces; after completing this chapter, you will be able to:

- Slice an image into several sprites (i.e., pieces).

- Shuffle the puzzle pieces.

- Make it possible for the player to move (i.e., drag and drop) these pieces.

- Make these pieces "snap" to a particular location.

- Detect when the player has dragged and dropped a piece to the correct location.

INTRODUCTION

Our complete game will look as follows:

- At the start the full puzzle is displayed to the left; the pieces are in the correct order.

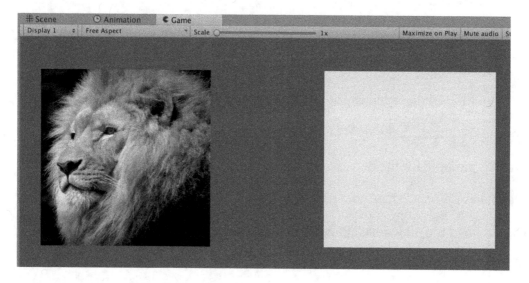

Figure 123: Overview of the game (part 1)

- After a few seconds, the pieces will be shuffled to add more challenge.

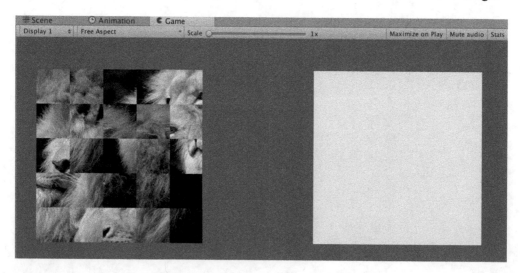

Figure 124: Overview of the game (part 2)

- The player will then need to drag and drop each of the pieces to the right location on the right panel.

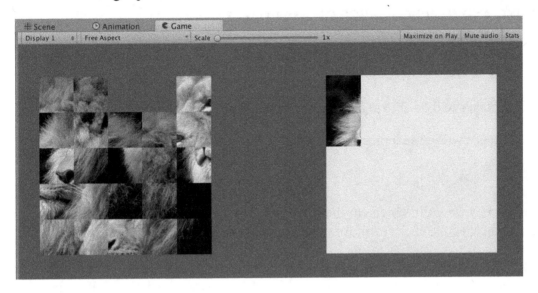

Figure 125: Overview of the game (part 3)

CREATING AND MOVING A PIECE OF THE PUZZLE

In this section, we will create a simple puzzle piece and make it possible for the player to drag and drop it:

- The player will be able to drag and drop this piece to a placeholder.

- The piece will be snapping to this placeholder, to make the game easier to use.

So let's get started.

In the next steps we will implement the **drag** function, which is the ability for the player to drag an object across the screen; for this, we will simply make sure that once the player drags the mouse over an object, that the position of the object is then the same as the position of the mouse. For this purpose, we will create a function that will be called every time an object is dragged (i.e., left click + move the mouse), and that will update the position of the object accordingly, so that it is exactly at the same as the position of the mouse, hence creating a dragging movement.

- Please save your current scene (**File | Save Scene**).

- Create a new scene (**File | New Scene**).

- Save your scene as **chapter4** (**File | Save Scene As**).

First, we can remove the sky background (if there is any in your current scene) using the menu **Window | Lighting**.

Then we can start to create a puzzle piece (i.e., an image) that we will be able to drag and drop.

- Please create a new **Image** (i.e., select **GameObject | UI | Image**) and rename it **image**.

- This will create a white square, as illustrated in the next figure.

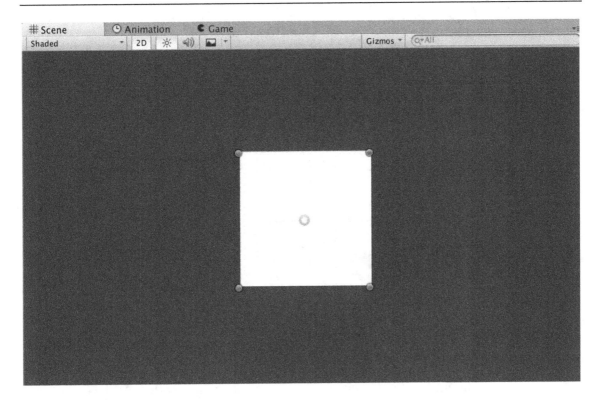

Figure 126: Creating a new image

We will now create a new script:

- Please create a new script called **DragAndDrop** (i.e., from the **Project** menu, select: **Create | C# Script**).

- Open this script (i.e., double click on the script **DragAndDrop** in the **Project** window).

- Add the following code to it (just before the end of the class).

```
public void Drag ()
{
    GameObject.Find("image").transform.position                    =
Input.mousePosition;
    print("Dragging" + gameObject.name);
}
```

In the previous code, the position of the object called **image** will be the same as the position of the mouse. This function will be called when the object is dragged.

- Please save this script, and add it (i.e., drag and drop it) to the object **image**.

- Select the object called **image** from the **Hierarchy**.

- Using the **Inspector**, add a component called **Event Trigger** (**Component | Event | Event Trigger**) to the object **image**.

- The following new component should now appear in the **Inspector** for the object image.

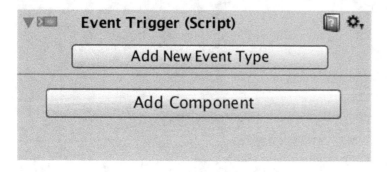

Figure 127: Adding an Event Trigger component (part 1)

- In the component **Event Trigger**, click on the button called **Add New Event Type** (as illustrated in the next figure) and then choose the option called **Drag** from the drop-down menu.

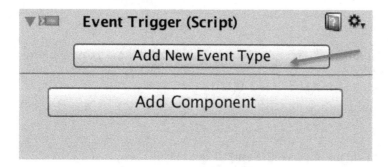

Figure 128: Adding an Event Trigger component (part 2)

- A new field called **Drag (BaseEventData)** should appear, as illustrated in the next figure.

- Please click on the + sign that is below the label **List is Empty**.

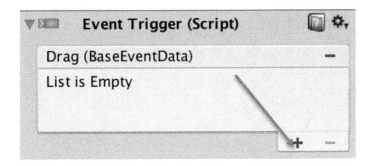

Figure 129: Configuring the new event (part1)

- This will create a new empty field with the label **None (Object)**.

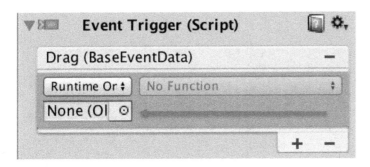

Figure 130:Configuring the new event (part 2)

- Drag and drop the object called **image** from the **Hierarchy** window to this field.

Figure 131: Configuring the new event (part 3)

- Next, you can click on the drop-down menu entitled **No Function**, and select **DragAndDrop | Drag**, as illustrated in the next figure.

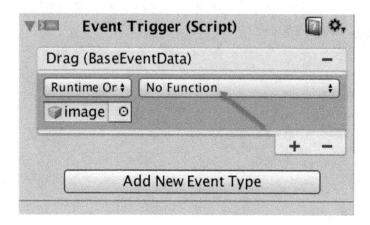

Figure 132: Configuring the new event (part 4)

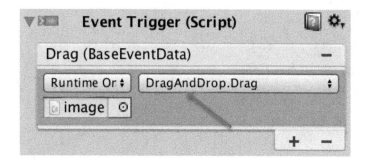

Figure 133: Configuring the new event (part 5)

You can now test your scene, and you should be able to drag the white square around the screen.

DROPPING THE TILE TO A PLACEHOLDER

Now that we can drag and drop the image, we will add a placeholder and modify our code so that the image snaps to the placeholder if it is dropped close enough.

The process will consist in:

- Creating a new image for the placeholder.

- Dropping the image near the placeholder.

- Checking the distance between the placeholder and the image.

- Placing the image atop the placeholder if the image is close enough.

- Placing the image back to its original position otherwise.

So let's proceed:

- Please create a new image (**Game Object | UI | Image**).

- Rename this image **PH1** (as in **P**lace**H**older **1**)

- Move this object **PH1** to the right of the object called **image**.

- Change the color of the object **PH1** to green, using the **Inspector**.

Figure 134: Adding a placeholder

Now that the placeholder (i.e., green square) has been created, we will create a new function in the script called **DragAndDrop**, that will be called when the user drops the image.

- Please open the script **DragAndDrop**.

- Add the following function at the end of the class.

```
public void Drop()
{
    GameObject ph1 = GameObject.Find("PH1");
    GameObject img = GameObject.Find("image");
    float  distance  =  Vector3.Distance(ph1.transform.position,
img.transform.position);
    if (distance <= 50)
    {
        img.transform.position = ph1.transform.position;
    }
}
```

In the previous code:

- We create two game objects that refer to the objects **image** and **PH1** that we have created earlier.

- We calculate the distance between the object called **image** and the object **PH1** (i.e., the placeholder).

- If this distance is less than 50, then the object called **image** is moved to the same position as the placeholder; this is the "snapping" effect that was mentioned earlier.

- Please save your code and check that it is error-free.

Now, we just need to add a new event to the object **image** to detect when the player drops (or stops dragging) the image; we will then link this event to the new function that we have just created (i.e., **Drop**).

- Please select the object called **image** in the **Hierarchy**.

- Using the **Inspector**, in the component called **Event Trigger**, click on the button called **Add New Event Type**.

Figure 135: Creating a new event (part 1)

- From the drop-down menu select the event called **End Drag**; this will create a new event, as illustrated on the next figure.

Figure 136: Creating a new event (part 2)

- Once this done, click on the drop-down menu to the right of the label **Runtime**, as illustrated in the next figure.

Figure 137: Creating a new event (part 2)

- From the drop-down menu, select: **DragAndDrop | Drop**, to indicate that, in case, the player stops dragging the image, then the function called **Drop** should be called.

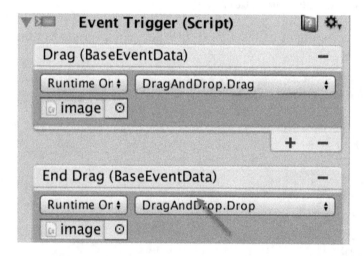

Figure 138: Creating a new event (part 3)

- Using the **Hierarchy**, you can also move (i.e., drag and drop) the object called **image** so that it is the second element listed within the object **Canvas**, as illustrated in the next figure; this is so that it is displayed atop the placeholder when dragged and dropped.

Figure 139: Moving the object image down the Hierarchy

You can now test your scene, and you should see that, as you drag and drop the image close to the placeholder, the image snaps to the placeholder.

Next, we will add code that will move the image back to its original position if it was dragged too far away from the placeholder.

- Please open the script called **DragAndDrop**.

- Add the following code at the beginning of the class.

```
Vector3 originalPosition;
```

- In the previous code, we declare a new variable that will be used to store the initial position of the image (i.e., before it was dragged).

- Modify the **Start** function as follows:

```
void Start ()
{
    originalPosition = transform.position;
}
```

- In the previous code, we record the initial position of the image and save it in the variable called **initialPosition**.

Next we will modify the function **Drag** to make our code more generic (and usable with other images later-on).

- Please, modify the function **Drag** as follows:

```
public void Drag()
{
    print ("Dragging");
    //GameObject.Find("Image").transform.position                    =
Input.mousePosition;
    gameObject.transform.position = Input.mousePosition;
}
```

In the previous code we comment the previous code and we also change the position of the object linked to this script.

Note that before you modify the function **Drop**, you can copy the code within, as we will be using this code in the function **checkMatch** later-on.

- Please modify the function **Drop** as follows:

```
public void Drop()
{
    checkMatch ();
}
```

In the previous code, when the image is dropped, we call a function named **checkMatch** that we yet have to define.

- Please add the function **checkMatch** at the end of the class, as follows:

```
public void checkMatch()
{
    GameObject ph1 = GameObject.Find ("PH1");
    GameObject img = GameObject.Find ("image");
    float distance = Vector3.Distance (ph1.transform.position,
img.transform.position);
    print ("Distance" + distance);
    if (distance <= 50)
        snap (img, ph1);
    else
        moveBack ();
}
```

In the previous code:

- This code is similar to the previous code in the **Drop** function.

- The only difference now is that if the image is close enough to the placeholder, we then call the function called **snap**, that we yet need to define, and that will snap the image to the placeholder.

- Otherwise, the function **moveBack** is called; this function, that we yet have to define, will move the image back to its original position.

So we just need to define these two new functions (i.e., **moveBack** and **snap**)

- Please add the function **moveBack**, as follows:

```
public void moveBack()
{
     transform.position = originalPosition;
}
```

In the previous code, we just move the image back to its original position.

We will now define the function **snap**.

- Please, add the function **snap**, as follows:

```
public void snap(GameObject img,GameObject ph )
{
     img.transform.position = ph.transform.position;
}
```

In the previous code:

- We define the function snap.

- It takes two **GameObject** parameters.

- It then sets the position of the first **GameObject** to the position of the second; so effectively, if the first parameter is the image, and the second parameter is the placeholder, it will snap the image to this particular placeholder.

Once this is done, you can test the **Scene**; as you drag and drop the image, it should snap to the placeholder, if you drag it close enough to the placeholder; otherwise, the image should be moved back to its original position.

USING MULTIPLE PLACEHOLDERS

So now that the snapping feature works, we will create multiple placeholders and check that the image snaps to the corresponding placeholder.

We will check that we are dropping the image on the right placeholder; for this, we will create a tag for the image; the name of the corresponding placeholder should then be **PH** followed by the corresponding tag (e.g., **PH1** for the image with the tag **1**, **PH2** for the image with the tag **2**, etc.).

- Please modify the function **checkMatch** as follows:

```
//GameObject ph1 = GameObject.Find ("PH1");
//GameObject img = GameObject.Find ("image");
GameObject img = gameObject;
string tag = gameObject.tag;
GameObject ph1 = GameObject.Find("PH" + tag);
```

In the previous code:

- We comment the first two lines that define the variables **ph1** and **img**.

- Instead, the variable **img** is now referring to the object linked to this script.

- The variable **ph1** (i.e., the corresponding placeholder) is then defined based on the tag of the image linked to this script.

Please save your code. We will now create the necessary tags.

- Please create a new tag called **1** (if you don't already have a tag with this name, based on the previous chapters).

- Assign the tag **1** to the object called **image**.

Figure 140: Adding a tag to the image

Creating a Puzzle Game

- Using the **Inspector**, check that the name of the placeholder is **PH1**.

- Duplicate the object **PH1**.

- Rename the duplicate **PH2**, and change its color to **red** (i.e., using the **Inspector**).

- Move the duplicate to the right of the green placeholder. The scene view should look like the next figure.

Figure 141: Creating a second placeholder

- Using the **Hierarchy**, you can also move (i.e., drag and drop) the object called **image** so that it is the third element listed within the object **Canvas**, as illustrated in the next figure; this is so that it is displayed atop the placeholders when dragged and dropped on them.

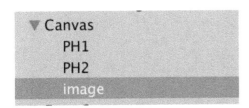

Figure 142: Moving down the image in the hierarchy

So, as the system is set-up, because the image has a tag called **1**, then its corresponding placeholder should be **PH1**, which is the green square. You can now test your scene and check that the image only snaps to the green placeholder, and that if you try to drag and drop it to the red box, that it is moved back to its original position.

Remember: because the **image** object has a tag called **1**, the corresponding placeholder is **PH1** (i.e., **PH** followed by the tag of the image).

USING AND SLICING A FULL IMAGE TO CREATE THE PUZZLE PIECES

Now that the drag and drop feature works we will start to create the visual aspect of the game, and create tiles for our puzzle, based on a main image.

- Please locate the image called **lion.png** in the resource pack.

- Import this image in **Unity** and rename it **lion**.

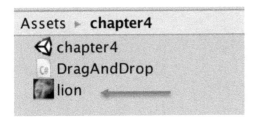

Figure 143: Importing the main image for the puzzle

- Select this asset (i.e., **lion**) in the **Project** window.

- Using the **Inspector** set its **Texture Type** to **Sprite (2D and UI)**, its **Sprite Mode** to **Multiple**, and its attribute **Pixels Per Unit** to **1000**, as per the next figure.

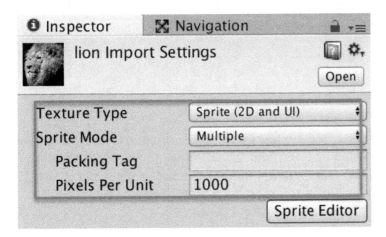

Figure 144: Setting the attributes of the image imported

- Once this is done, you can press the **Apply** button, located in the bottom-right corner of the **Inspector**.

Figure 145: Applying changes

Once this is done, we will slice this image in individual cells that will make-up the pieces of the puzzle.

- Using the **Inspector** window, click on the button called **Sprite Editor**, as illustrated in the next figure.

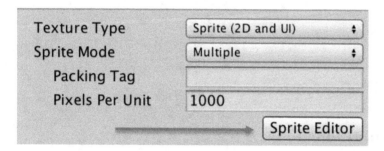

Figure 146: Modifying the image's properties

- In the new window, click on the button called **Slice** located in the top-left corner.

Figure 147: Slicing the image

- In the new window, please select the option **Grid by Cell count** for the attribute **Type**, and then specify a value of **5** for both the attributes **C** and **R**, as illustrated in the next figure This means that we want to slice the main image and create 25 images (5 by 5) based on a grid of 5 columns and 5 rows.

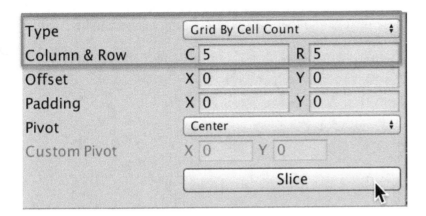

Figure 148: Specifying the slicing options

- Once this is done, you can click on the button called **Slice**.

- You should then see that the image is part of a grid, as illustrated in the next figure.

Figure 149: Creating the new grid

Now, we just need to apply these changes so that the corresponding pieces can be created.

- You can click on the button called **Apply**, located in the top-right corner of the screen.

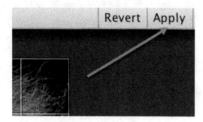

Figure 150: Applying changes

- Once this is done, if you look at the **Project** window, you should see that the image **lion** has turned into a folder were **25 sprites** have been created (e.g., **lion_0**, **lion_1**, **lion_2**, etc.). These new sprites are effectively the cells of the grid that we have defined earlier in the **Sprite Editor**.

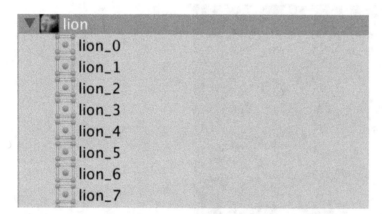

Figure 151: The 25 pieces have been created

Next, we will add the code that will create objects (i.e., puzzle pieces) based on these new sprites.

- Please close the **Sprite Editor** window.

- Using the **Hierarchy** window, please change the name of the object called **image** to **piece** (i.e., its new name should be **piece**).

- Create a prefab from it (i.e., drag and drop the object **piece** to the **Project** window).

- This prefab should automatically be named **piece**, as illustrated in the next figure.

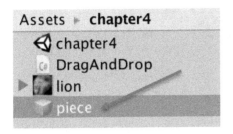

Figure 152: Creating a new prefab

- Please duplicate the object called **piece** and rename the duplicate **piece2**; change its tag to **2** (you may need to create a new tag called **2** prior to that).

- Using the **Hierarchy**, move the object called **piece2** slightly above the object **piece**.

- Select the object called **piece**.

- Using the **Hierarchy**, you should see that it includes a component called **Image** with an attribute called **Source Image**.

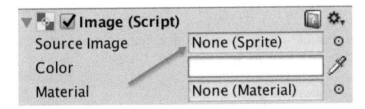

Figure 153: Checking the Image component

- Please drag and drop the image **lion_0** from the **Project** window, to the field **Source Image** for the object **piece**, as illustrated in the next figure.

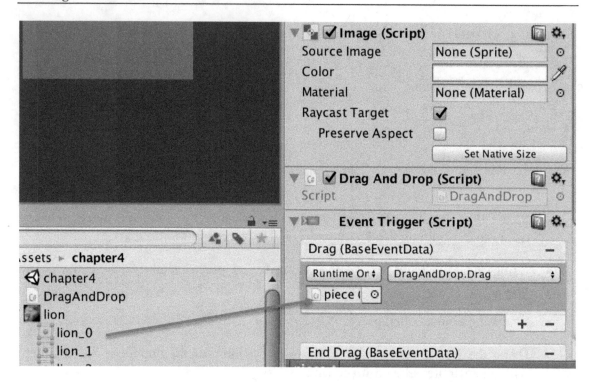

- Please repeat the last step so that the image **lion_1** is dragged from the **Project** window, to the field **Source Image** of the component called **Image**, for the object **piece2** this time.

- Once this is done, the **Scene** view may look as follows:

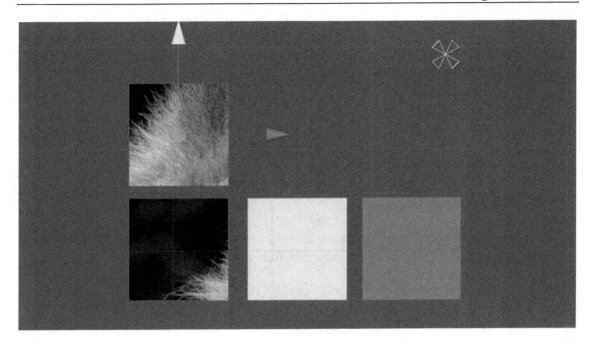

Figure 154: Adding texture to pieces

You can now play the scene and test that the first piece only snaps to the first placeholder, and that the second piece only snaps to the second placeholder.

GENERATING SPRITES AT RUN-TIME

At this stage the snapping of each image is working; so next, we will generate all the pieces of the puzzle from our code, along with the placeholders where they should be dropped to.

- Please create a new empty object (**GameObject | Create Empty**) called **managePuzzleGame**.

- From the **Project** window, create a new script called **ManagePuzzleGame** and link it (i.e., drag and drop) to the object **managePuzzleGame**.

- Create an empty text object (i.e., **GameObject | UI | Text**) called **centerOfTheScreen** located in the middle of the screen (i.e., PosX=0 and PosY=0 for the component **RectTransform**). Please make sure that its text is empty.

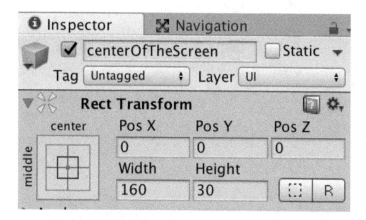

Figure 155: Centering the text object

- Duplicate this object (i.e., **centerOfTheScreen**) twice to create an object called **leftSide** located halfway between the object **centerOTheScreen** and the left edge of the white rectangle, and an object called **rightSide** located halfway between the object **centerOfTheScreen** and the right edge of the white rectangle.

- The position of these three **UI Text** object, could be as illustrated in the next figure.

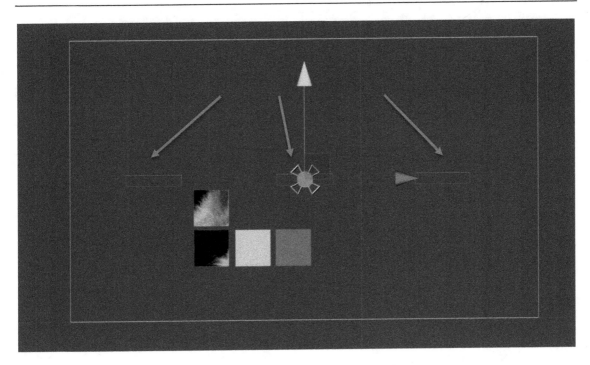

Figure 156: Adding invisible markers

- Using the **Hierarchy** window, create a prefab from the object called **PH1**, and rename this prefab **PH**.

- You can also create additional tags, as we have done before, so that your tags range from **1** to **25**; these tags will be used for the 25 pieces of the puzzle.

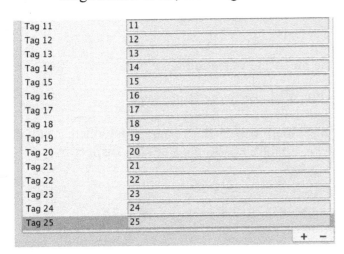

Figure 157: Creating 25 tags

Once this done, we can start to work on the script **ManagePuzzleGame**.

- Please open the script **ManagePuzzleGame**.

- Add this code at the beginning of the class.

```
using UnityEngine.UI;
public class ManagePuzzleGame : MonoBehaviour {
    public Image piece;
    public Image placeHolder;
    float phWidth, phHeight;
```

In the previous code:

- We include the **UI** library that will be used to gain access to **UI** elements from our script (i.e., text fields); we also declare three variables. Two of these variables are **public** which means that they will be accessible from outside the script, including from the **Inspector**.

- The variable **piece** will be used for an image template to be employed for each piece of the puzzle.

- The variable **placeholder** will be used for an image template to be employed for each placeholder (where the pieces have to be dragged and dropped to).

- The variables **phWidth** and **PhHeight** will refer to the width and height of the placeholder.

Please save your code.

- We can now initialize the variable **piece** and **placeholder**:

- Please select the object **ManagePuzzleGame** in the **Hierarchy**.

- You should see, using the **Inspector**, that the component called **managePuzzleGame** has now two variables accessible from the **Inspector**.

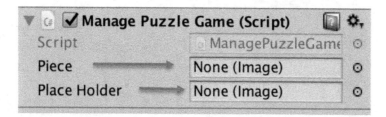

- Please drag and drop the prefab **piece** and **PH** from the **Project** window to the fields **piece** and **placeholder**, respectively, as illustrated in the next figure.

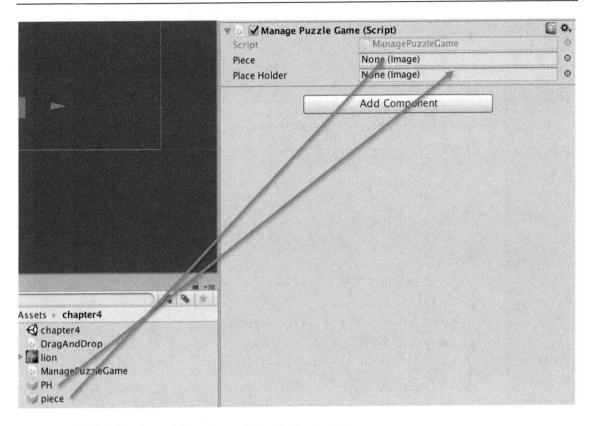

Figure 158: Initializing the variables piece and placeholder (part 1)

- The **Inspector** should then look as the next figure.

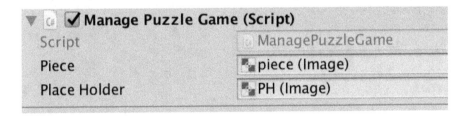

Figure 159: Initializing the variables piece and placeholder (part 2)

We will now modify the script **ManagePuzzleGame** to create the necessary placeholders for the game, based on the prefab **PH**.

- Please open the script **ManagePuzzleGame**.

- Modify the **Start** function as follows:

```
void Start ()
{
    createPlaceHolders ();
}
```

- Add the following function at the end of the class.

```
public void createPlaceHolders()
{
    phWidth = 100; phHeight = 100;
    float nbRows, nbColumns;
    nbRows = 5;
    nbColumns = 5;
    for (int i = 0; i < 25; i++)
    {
        Vector3 centerPosition = new Vector3 ();
        centerPosition                  =              GameObject.Find
("rightSide").transform.position;
        float row, column;
        row = i % 5;
        column = i / 5;
        Vector3 phPosition = new Vector3 (centerPosition.x +
phWidth*(row-nbRows/2), centerPosition.y - phHeight * (column-
nbColumns/2), centerPosition.z);
        Image   ph    =    (Image)(Instantiate    (placeHolder,
phPosition, Quaternion.identity));
        ph.tag = ""+(i + 1);
        ph.name = "PH"+(i + 1);
        ph.transform.SetParent(GameObject.Find
("Canvas").transform);
    }
}
```

In the previous code:

- We set the width and height of all placeholders.

- We then define that the placeholders (i.e., where the puzzle pieces should be dropped to) consist of a grid of 5 rows by 5 columns.

- We then go through this grid, row by row.

- The row and column numbers are defined by dividing **i** (which ranges from **1 to 25**) by **5** or by saving the remainder of this division.

- For example if **i=12** , the row will be **2** (i.e., the **quotient** of **12/5**) and the column will be 2 (the **remainder of 12/10,** noted as **12%2**).

- The position of each placeholder is based on these calculations

- We set the tag of the placeholder.

- We also specify that the parent of each placeholder is the object called **Canvas**; this is necessary so that the placeholder can be displayed through our canvas.

- All the new objects are centred around the object **rightSide**.

Please save your code and play the scene; you should see that 25 placeholders have been created.

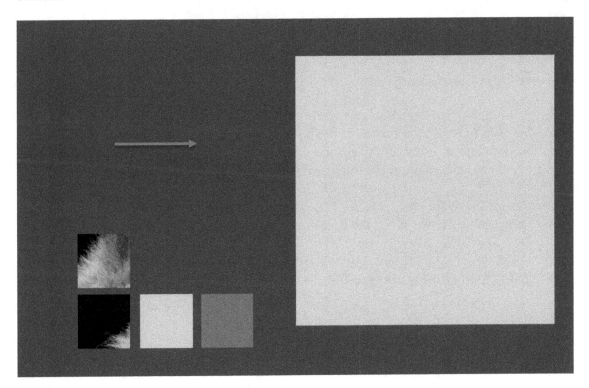

Figure 160: The new placeholders in the game view

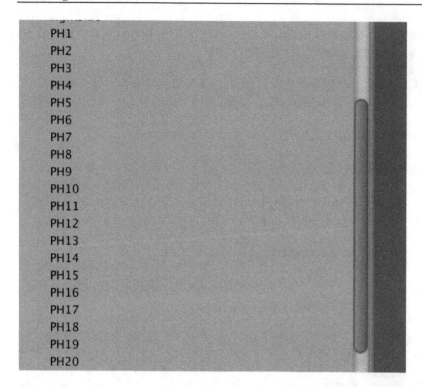

PH1
PH2
PH3
PH4
PH5
PH6
PH7
PH8
PH9
PH10
PH11
PH12
PH13
PH14
PH15
PH16
PH17
PH18
PH19
PH20

Figure 161: The new placeholders in the Hierarchy view

Next, we need to create the pieces of the puzzle; to do so, we will use the sprites created from the **lion** image; however, while these sprites are now in the folder called **lion**, we will move these to the **Resources** folder, so that they can be accessed from our script.

- Using the **Inspector**, select all the images under the folder **lion** (i.e., the sprites generated after we sliced the **lion** image)

- Drag and drop them to the folder called **Resources** (if you don't have this folder yet in your project, you can create it using **Create | Folder**).

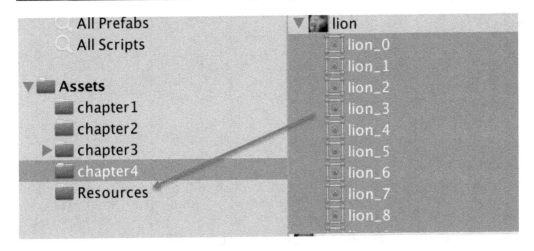

Figure 162: Moving the images to the Resources folder

Next, we will create the code to generate the puzzle pieces from our script.

- Please add the following code to the class **ManagePuzzleGame**.

```
public void createPieces()
{
    phWidth = 100;
    phHeight = 100;
    float nbRows, nbColumns;
    nbRows = 5;
    nbColumns = 5;

}
```

In the previous code, we use the same code as we have done earlier for the placeholders to define the size of each image (i.e., **phWidth** and **phHeight**), along with the size of the grid used to display these images (i.e., **nbRows** and **nbColumns**).

- Please, add the following code at the end of the function **createPieces**.

```
for (int i = 0; i < 25; i++)
{
    Vector3 centerPosition = new Vector3 ();
    centerPosition                    =           GameObject.Find
("leftSide").transform.position;
    float row, column;
    row = i % 5;
    column = i / 5;
    Vector3 phPosition = new Vector3 (centerPosition.x + phWidth
* (row - nbRows / 2), centerPosition.y - phHeight * (column -
nbColumns / 2), centerPosition.z);
    Image  ph  =  (Image)(Instantiate  (piece,  phPosition,
Quaternion.identity));
    ph.tag = "" + (i + 1);
    ph.name = "Piece" + (i + 1);
    ph.transform.SetParent(GameObject.Find
("Canvas").transform);
    Sprite[] allSprites = Resources.LoadAll<Sprite> ("lion");
    Sprite s1 = allSprites [i];
    ph.GetComponent<Image> ().sprite = s1;

}
```

In the previous code:

- The previous code is very similar to the code that we have created in the function **createPlaceholders**; the only difference being that…

- The images are centered around the object called **leftSide**.

- The images used for each piece are from the folder called **Resources**.

Please save your code.

- You can now deactivate the objects **PH**, **PH2**, **piece**, and **piece2** in the **Hierarchy**.

- We can also add the following code to the **Start** function (new code in bold) in the script **ManagePuzzleGame**.

```
void Start ()
{
    createPlaceHolders ();
    createPieces ();
}
```

- Please save your code, and play the scene; it should look as follows:

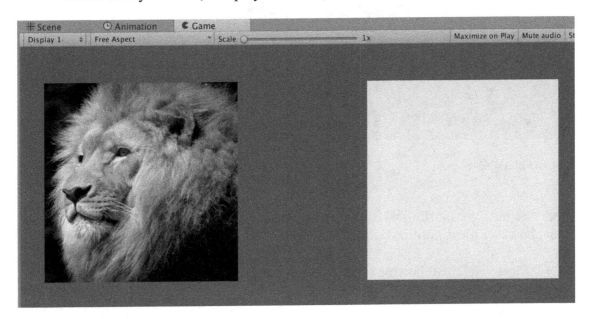

Figure 163: Displaying the start of the game

- You can also try to drag and drop pieces from the left to their correct location on the board to the right.

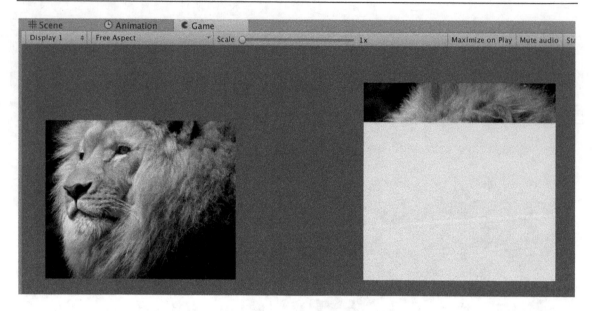

Figure 164: Testing the game

Next, we need to shuffle the cards; their values (i.e., tags or images) will remain the same; however, their position will be changed, in order to challenge the player.

- Please add the following function to the script **ManagePuzzleGame**.

```
void shufflePieces()
{
    int[] newArray = new int [25];
    for (int i = 0; i < 25; i++)
    newArray [i] = i;
    int tmp;
    for (int t = 0; t < 25; t++ )
    {
        tmp = newArray[t];
        int r = Random.Range(t, 10);
        newArray[t] = newArray[r];
        newArray[r] = tmp;
    }
    for (int i = 0; i < 25; i++)
    {
        float row, nbRows, nbColumns, column;
        nbRows = 5;
        nbColumns = 5;
        row = (newArray[i]) % 5;
        column = (newArray[i]) / 5;
        Vector3 centerPosition = new Vector3 ();
        centerPosition               =               GameObject.Find
("leftSide").transform.position;
        var g = GameObject.Find("Piece"+(i + 1));
        Vector3 newPosition = new Vector3 (centerPosition.x +
phWidth*(row-nbRows/2), centerPosition.y - phHeight * (column-
nbColumns/2), centerPosition.z);
        g.transform.position = newPosition;
    }
}
```

In the previous code:

- We create an array of 25 integers.

- We then initialize this array so that its values are ranked from 0 to 24.

- We then use a loop to shuffle the values in this array.

- The random numbers are saved in the array called **newArray**.

- Once this is done, we use another loop where we modify the position of each of the pieces onscreen, using the random numbers generated earlier (the array **newArray**).

Once this is done, we can add the following code at the end of the **Start** function

```
shufflePieces();
```

- Please, save your code and test the scene; you should see that the pieces have been shuffled.

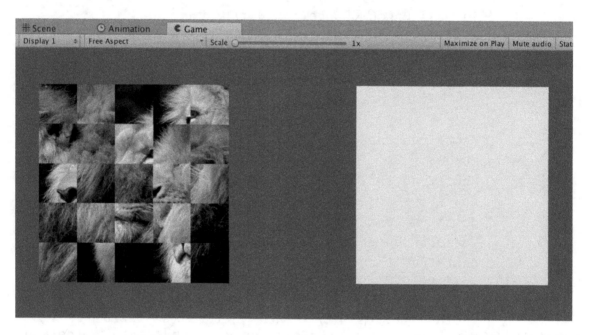

Figure 165: Displaying shuffled pieces

The last thing we could do is to make sure that the user can see the completed puzzle before the pieces are shuffled. To do so, we will include a delay just before the pieces are shuffled.

- Please add this code at the beginning of the class:

```
float timer;
bool cardsShuffled = false;
```

- Modify the **Start** function to comment the shuffle function as follows (new code in bold):

```
void Start () {
createPlaceHolders ();
createPieces ();
//shufflePieces ();
```

- Modify the **Update** function as follows:

```
void Update ()
{
        timer += Time.deltaTime;
        if (timer >= 4 && !cardsShuffled) {
                shufflePieces ();
                cardsShuffled = true;
        }
}
```

In the previous code:

- We create a timer.

- This timer's value will increase every seconds.

- 4 seconds after the game has started, the pieces are shuffled.

- We then set the variable **cardsShuffled** to true so that the card shuffling happens only once.

Last but not least, we need to set the initial position of each piece after they have been shuffled as follows:

- Please open the script **DragAndDrop** and add the following function to it:

```
public void initCardPosition()
{
        originalPosition = transform.position;
}
```

- Save your script, then open the class **ManagePuzzleGame**.

- Modify the function **shufflePieces** as follows (new code in bold):

```
g.transform.position = newPosition;
g.GetComponent<DragAndDrop> ().initCardPosition ();
```

You can now save your code and play the scene; as the game starts, the player will have 4 seconds to look at the completed puzzle before the cards are shuffled.

Note that if you see a warning message saying "**Parent of RectTransform is being set with parent property. Consider using the SetParent method instead, with the worldPositionStays argument set to false.**", you can change the following code in the class **ManagePuzzleGame**.

```
ph.transform.parent = GameObject.Find ("Canvas").transform;
```

to...

```
ph.transform.SetParent(GameObject.Find ("Canvas").transform);
```

LEVEL ROUNDUP

Summary

In this chapter, we have managed to create a challenging puzzle game where the player has to memorize an image, before trying to complete the puzzle; we have learnt some interesting skills along the way, including: dragging and dropping objects, snapping sprites to placeholders, shuffling images, creating a timer, slicing an image, and creating sprites based on a grid layout.

Checklist

You can consider moving to the next stage if you can do the following:

- Understand how to access sprites from a script.

- Understand how to create an array of integers.

- Know how to create and process drag and drop events .

Quiz

Now, let's check your knowledge! Please answer the following questions (the answers are included in the resource pack) or specify whether they are correct or incorrect.

1. To select all the assets in a given folder, you can just press **CTRL + A**.

2. To be able to detect that a sprite was dragged, this sprite needs to have a collider component.

3. The component **Event Trigger** can be used to detect events such as drag or drop.

4. To create an empty object, you can select: **GameObject | Create | Empty Object**.

5. In Unity, it is possible to use tags that have been created in other scenes (but in the same project).

6. The sprite editor can be used to slice images.

7. Images can be sliced based on a grid (column and rows).

8. When an image is sliced, all the sub-images created are automatically added to the folder **Resources**.

9. The following code will save all sprites stored in the folder called **lion** to the array called **allSprites**.

```
Sprite[] allSprites = Resources.LoadAll<Sprite> ("lion");
```

10. The following code will create an array of 10 integers.

```
int [] newArray = new int [] {0,1,2,3,4,5,6,7,8,9};
```

Challenge 1

For this chapter, your challenge will be to modify the game as follows:

- Detect when the puzzle has been completed.
- Create a button to restart the game.

5
FREQUENTLY ASKED QUESTIONS

This chapter provides answers to the most frequently asked questions about the features that we have covered in this book. Please also note that some <u>videos are also available on the companion site</u> to help you with some of the concepts covered in this book.

ACCESSING RESOURCES

Where should I store assets if I want to access them from a script?

You can create a folder called **Resources**, and then save your imported assets in this folder.

How can I access a text file that I have saved in the Resources folder?

To access this file (and the text within) you can use the following code snippet.

```
TextAsset        t1       =        (TextAsset)Resources.Load("words",
typeof(TextAsset));
string s = t1.text;
```

How can I access an image file that I have saved in the Resources folder?

To access an individual sprite from the **Resources** folder, you can use the following code snippet.

```
Sprite s1 = (Sprite) (Resources.Load<Sprite>(nameOfCard));
```

However, if you'd prefer to access and save several sprites at once, then you can use the following snippet:

```
Sprite[] allSprites = Resources.LoadAll<Sprite> ("lion");
```

DETECTING USER INPUTS

How can I detect keystrokes?

You can detect keystrokes by using the function **Input.GetKey**. For example, the following code detects when the key **E** is pressed; this code should be added to the **Update** function.

```
If (Input.GetKey(KeyCode.E)){...}
```

How can I detect a click on a button?

To detect clicks on a button, you can do the following:

- Create an empty object.

- Create a new script and link it to this object.

- Select the button in the **Hierarchy**.

- Using the **Inspector**, click on the button located below the label called **OnClick**.

- Drag and drop the empty object to the field that just appeared.

- From the **Inspector**, you should then be able to select the function that should be called in case the button is clicked.

How can I detect drag and drop events on an image?

To detect drag and drop events or actions on an image:

- Select the image from the **Hierarchy**.

- Using the **Inspector**, add a component called **Event   Trigger   (Component | Event | Event Trigger)** to this image.

- In the component **Event   Trigger**, click on the button called **Add   New   Event   Type**   (as illustrated in the next figure) and then choose the option called **Drag   or   End Drag** from the drop-down menu.

6
THANK YOU

I would like to thank you for completing this book; I trust that you are now comfortable with creating simple 2D puzzle games. This book is the third in the series "A Beginner's Guide to" that covers particular aspects of Unity, so it may be time to move on to the next books where you will get started with even more specific features. You can find a description of these forthcoming books on the official page http://www.learntocreategames.com/books/.

In case you have not seen it yet, you can subscribe to our Facebook group using the following link; it includes a community of like-minded game creators who share ideas and are ready to help you with your game projects.

http://facebook.com/groups/learntocreategames/

You may also subscribe to our mailing list to receive weekly updates and information on how to create games and improve your skills.

http://learntocreategames.com/2d-platform-games/

So that the book can be constantly improved, I would really appreciate your feedback. So, please leave me a helpful review on Amazon letting me know what you thought of the book and also send me an email (learntocreategames@gmail.com) with any suggestions you may have. I read and reply to every email.

Thanks so much!!